PAT —

GOOD LUCK AND

GOD BLESS!

LIVE, LOVE, LAUGH!

BILL CLARKE

DEC. 2014

Retirement Renaissance

A New Look at Retirement Planning
Through the Eyes of a Veteran Retiree
by
William L. Clarke

Independent Publisher Services
www.publisherservices-us.com
ISBN: 978-1-61623-893-3
Retirement Renaissance™ is a Registered Trademark
William L. Clarke, August 2009

ISBN 978-1-61623-893-3

90000>

9 781616 238933

Notice
Mention of specific organizations or authorities in the book
does not imply endorsement by either the author or
publisher or by the organizations or authorities
mentioned or quoted in the book.
Internet addresses provided in the book were accurate
at the time the book was published.
Contact and Ordering Information:
www.retirementren.com
info@retirementren.com

About the Book
Bill Clarke, a Veteran Retiree

 When I started to write *Retirement Renaissance,* I was trying to figure out why I wasn't totally enthused with retirement. My expectations of retirement did not match my feelings. I began to realize that my job and career had been far more important to my psychological wellbeing than I had imagined. I missed the sense of satisfaction and the feeling of contribution that was a routine part of my daily business life. I missed my colleagues. I missed the sights and sounds of the business arena. In short, I realized I had left something that I really enjoyed. I was disenchanted because I had not replaced the psychological requirements that my job had provided. It was from these early feelings that I developed the motivation to explore the realm of retirement planning. I read numerous books about retirement planning. I quickly learned that most books on the subject deal almost exclusively with financial planning and my problem was more practical; I needed to find a true, comprehensive retirement plan. When I couldn't find the answers, I decided to see if I could figure it out on my own. I was a management consultant by profession so I saw it as an opportunity to solve a problem. I plunged into the project and many months later the result was the *Retirement Renaissance.*

You have the opportunity to do whatever you want to do in retirement. The most important thing is that you have to plan for what you want to do, especially how to deal with the psychological loss of your job and career and the sense of wellbeing and self-esteem it provided. Retirement will not wait for you, it will happen whether you are prepared or not. Just follow my advice and prepare a retirement plan, with your spouse or partner. I guarantee that you will thank me in a few years from now. Incidentally, after I wrote the book, I decided to go back to work, part-time, because I really enjoyed my work. My present guideline about work is that I will continue as long as two conditions are present; first, that my clients think that I add value; and second, and that I am willing to roll out of bed in the morning and go to work. When either or both of these guidelines aren't there, I will retire, again.

Testimonials for *Retirement Renaissance*

"Some retirees drift into retirement without a particular plan about how they will spend their time. After reading *Retirement Renaissance*, I can now understand that I will get out of retirement what I plan to get out of it. Thanks for providing the insights that come from someone who has truly been there and done that."
~Michael Levy, Ph.D., Charles Clarke Reynolds Professor of Marketing, Babson College, Babson Park, MA

"*Retirement Renaissance* identifies trends that are beginning to shape the new age of retirement planning. It opened my eyes to the need for a personal plan to balance my wants and needs in the more simple years. With gratitude for this guidebook that is now at the center of my retirement planning toolkit."
~J. Kay Tormey, President, Samaritan Health Foundation, Dayton

"It was refreshing to read how the concept of retirement is changing and that I can write my own rules about when I retire or if I retire in a traditional sense. I now see retirement as purely a personal option and Bill Clarke hit the nail on the head in describing how work and personal life are merging into a new integrated lifestyle that may eliminate the need or desire to ever retire."
~N. Karl Haden, Ph.D., President, Academy for Academic Leadership, Atlanta, GA

"When I look back over my career, Bill is one of the people who provided valuable guidance and friendship to me many times and continues to do it as I approach retirement. If you thought you were prepared for retirement, take another look and read *Retirement Renaissance*. Bill Clarke proves that the best and most sage advice about retirement comes from those who are already retired. Heed his advice and read about what you need to do to ensure a long and happy retirement experience."
~Jim Sage, Vice President Information Technology and CIO, The University of Akron

"What a refreshing and useful book about the many and unanticipated challenges of the retirement process! Financial planning is not retirement planning—it's only a part of it! All retirees and retiree wannabes can benefit by reading *Retirement Renaissance*."
~*Peter Carusone, Professor Emeritus, Wright State University, Dayton, OH*

"Bill Clarke is "on the mark" with this book. Retirement is a wonderful opportunity to open new vistas. His approach can turn uncertainty and confusion for those facing retirement into a successful and fulfilling experience."
~*William M. Bennett, Retired Vice Chairman, Bank One Columbus, Columbus, OH*

"*Retirement Renaissance* is a timely read for someone who is not yet retired and needs to understand what retirement is all about. The concept of a personalized retirement plan resonated well with me because at this point in my life I am not sure if I really want to retire in a traditional sense. It is obvious that this veteran retiree walks the walk and talks the talk when it comes to managing a successful retirement."
~*Jim Sankey, President & CEO, InVue Security Products, Inc., Charlotte, NC*

"I have known Bill Clarke for thirty years; first, as a professional colleague, soaking in his wisdom about how to adapt my company to an ever-changing business environment and then as a friend, a condition one could not avoid when spending any amount of time in his presence. Bill's own life experience is all about adaptation to change and challenges both professionally and most importantly, personally. The book shows us how to adapt to our retirement years and how to "do" retirement right."
~*Joe Bressi, Retired Senior Vice President, Camelot Music (national music store chain), Canton, OH*

"In my experience as a retired financial executive, I can assure you that financial planning is essential but more important is determining what you want and need to do with your time to ensure a satisfying and rewarding retirement. *Retirement Renaissance* is the first book I've read that focuses on the whole life experience of retirement."
~*Dick Stilley, Retired CFO, Halls Merchandising, a division of Hallmark Cards, Kansas City, MO*

"I have known Bill and his wife Patty for over fifty years and remember the day when he called and informed me that their first child Christopher had been born with severe handicaps. This positive courage learned way back then exudes itself throughout the pages of his book and reveals the wisdom that comes from learning how to prevail over the challenges of life."
~Rev. Dr. Norbert C. Burns, S.M., Professor Emeritus, University of Dayton

"Retirement planning is much more involved that simply getting your finances in order. Bill Clarke hit the nail on the head that most retirement plans focus only on financial planning and leave out all the other things that are a part of daily retirement life."
~Fran Millar, Senior Vice President, Wells Fargo Insurance Services USA, Inc., Georgia State Representative, Atlanta, GA

"Kudos to *Retirement Renaissance*. As an academic nearing retirement, the book provided an excellent overview of all the things a future retiree needs to consider before they retire. After reading the book and learning about the changing retirement paradigm, I am not at all sure that I will ever retire totally. I like the idea of integrating my career activities with my personal lifestyle. We seniors have spent several decades developing our skills and it doesn't seem right to abandon them suddenly when they provide the primary source of our personal satisfaction and fulfillment."
~Charlene R. Williams, Ph.D., Acting Chair, Division of Business, Brewton-Parker College, Mt. Vernon, GA

Acknowledgements

There are so many people who made this book possible. I relied heavily on the advice of my family, close friends, business associates, and golfing buddies. All of you helped to confirm two important issues; first, the best sources for insights about retirement are the seniors who are already retired; and second, most seniors do not spend enough time on the non-financial aspects of retirement planning. As a result, a great many seniors go into retirement unprepared for what they face in the early days and months of retirement. My purpose in writing this book was to provide a way for all retirees to anticipate and plan for all aspects of the retirement experience. Thanks to everyone for your patience and valuable advice.

I would like to especially thank my wife, Patty, my lifelong partner and best friend, for putting up with my craziness as I labored oblivious at times of her personal needs. I apologize for the late dinners, the lost time together, the many nights I crept into my study at 3:00am to capture the latest idea. She has been a true gift over all these many married years and especially now. I love you, sweet wife of mine.

There was a time when I almost trashed the project as I grew weary of the difficulty that an unpublished author has in getting the attention of literary agents and publishers. Had it not been for the words of encouragement from N. Karl Haden, Ph.D., friend and colleague, I might not have finished the project. Karl is President of the Academy for Academic Leadership (www.academicleaders.org)

A special thanks to my supporting cast that provided technical assistance in bringing the book to print, especially Neal Berry and Mike Weisenborn, Partners with Clearbuilt Technologies (www.clearbuilt.com) for their help in getting the book ready for printing. Finally, to my new friends at Independent Publisher Services, especially Brenda Rachal for guidance and Jaime Presail for the cover design, thank you for helping a novice.

My hope is that everyone who has been a part of this effort will be pleased and proud of the final product. Thank you so very much.

~Bill Clarke, Author

CONTENTS

Page

Section One—A New Look at Retirement Planning

Chapter 1
History of Retirement

Chapter 2
The Changing World of Retirement
Impact of the Global Economic Recession
Influence of the Baby Boomers
Technology and the Nature of Work
New Retirement Paradigm
Financial Planning vs. Retirement Planning
Potential Insolvency of the Social Security System

Chapter 3
A Better Name for Retirement?
A Look into the Future of Retirement

Chapter 4
Retirement in Perspective
Transition from Need to Want
Reward Yourself
Achieve Fulfillment
Personal Fulfillment
Common Characteristics of Happy Retirees
Secret to Achieving Fulfillment

Business and Career
Church and Spiritual
Community
Organizations and Clubs

Music
Painting and Art
Hobbies and Crafts

Introduction

"Twenty years from now you will be more disappointed by the things you didn't do than by the ones you did do. So throw off the bowlines. Sail away from the safe harbor. Catch the trade winds in your sails. Explore. Dream. Discover."

~ Mark Twain

Just about all books on "retirement planning" deal with the financial aspects of retirement. This book is different because it looks at retirement planning from a *whole life or total* perspective and provides a comprehensive series of steps to ensure that a prospective or recent retiree covers all the issues that need to be considered when planning for retirement. Financial planning is important but more important is the need to understand what retirement is all about.

Retirement Renaissance is organized into three sections:

1. A New Look at Retirement Planning
2. Personalized Retirement Plan (PRP)
3. Insights and Words of Wisdom

Section one explains the conditions and trends that all retirees need to understand about contemporary retirement planning. The second section provides a brief overview of the ten steps that comprise the Personalized Retirement Plan. The third section is a summation of the advice, wisdom and counsel learned from talking to hundreds of current retirees. Finally, the concluding chapter introduces a new concept called the Wisdom Corps that represents enormous potential for future generations of retirees.

Here is what the first section; **A New Look at Retirement Planning** is all about.

The Retirement Renaissance

There is a *renaissance* beginning to occur with traditional retirement planning. There are several conditions or trends that are triggering the renaissance. Every retiree needs to understand these issues because they will have enormous impact on current and future retirement plans.

❑ **Impact of the Global Economic Recession**—the sudden and precipitous drop in the financial market has caused many seniors to delay their retirement plans or possibly eliminate the dream of a traditional retirement. For those already retired, it means some serious belt-tightening and possibly the need to return to work, full or part-time.

❑ **Influence of the Baby Boomers**—the 78 million Baby Boomers that are just beginning their retirement years are younger, more active, healthier, and far less traditional/ The combination of all these attributes and attitudes is creating a new and different way of looking at retirement.

❑ **A New Retirement Paradigm**—Boomers are challenging the existing paradigm about when to retire, what to do in retirement, or whether to retire at all in a traditional sense. The new paradigm views retirement more as an option than a career end goal or personal requirement.

❑ **Technology and the Nature of Work**—the nature and process of work will continue to change as technology impacts how and where work is performed and to integrate work and personal lifestyle into one, inseparable continuum of activity.

❑ **Financial Planning vs. Retirement Planning**—the traditional process of preparing a retirement plan has historically focused on financial planning. As a result, many retirees stumble into retirement with a financial plan but not a clue as to what they want or need to do to create a truly satisfying retirement experience.

❑ **Health of the Social Security System**—many experts predict that the Social Security trust fund and Medicare Hospital Insurance trust fund will run out of money if left on the current track. There is almost unanimous consensus that a crisis is pending that represents a major impending disaster for millions of dependent retirees.

Retirement Redefined

This chapter looks at the concept of retirement and the word itself that implies a moving away from something rather than the beginning of a new life experience. Perhaps the name *retirement* should have a meaning more like a graduation *commencement* that puts a positive spin on a new and exciting time of life. The author believes the new name for retirement should be *renaissance* to imply a new way, a time of change and innovation.

Purpose of Retirement

Not too many retirees start their retirement experience with a preplanned purpose in mind. They just sort of embark on their journey with the intent of having fun and enjoying life. Yet every other part of one's life has a purpose. While in school, our purpose was to get a quality education. During our career, the purpose was to learn a skill and earn a comfortable living. With our family, the purpose was to develop and nurture our children.

If all other parts of our lives have a purpose, then there is a need to have a primary purpose for retirement. The author suggests that a highly noble purpose is to achieve personal or self-fulfillment for a life well spent.

The Post-Retirement Syndrome

An issue that few retirees are prepared for is the potential to experience a serious psychological adjustment to retirement. Nobody likes to talk about it because retirement is supposed to be a time of happiness and personal satisfaction. Instead, some retirees experience a "post-retirement syndrome" that is triggered by the loss of one's job and career.

The basis for the syndrome is a failure to anticipate the importance that our job and career played in creating a sense of accomplishment and self-worth. When the job and career ends and is not replaced with something that provides a similar level of psychological comfort, the retiree is likely to experience depression. The key is to anticipate the potential problem and plan for doing things that replace the psychological need.
\
The second section of the book, **Personalized Retirement Plan (PRP),** introduces the need for a complete and comprehensive approach for preparing a retirement plan. The PRP consists of ten steps that deal with all the issues and concerns that a retiree needs to consider in preparing a retirement plan. Each step is explained in detail and the key issues are summarized at the end of each chapter in a series of key questions.

The fact is that no one is ever totally prepared for retirement. Although most major companies and institutions have some sort of an "on-boarding" process for new employees, few organizations have an effective "out-boarding" process to prepare a retiree for what they will experience.

Apparently society in general thinks that retirement is a "no brainer" and something that will come naturally. There are many retirees who now understand, through trial and error, that retirement is something that requires an organized approach to determine what you want or need to do to enjoy and prosper in your retirement years.

The ten steps within the PRP are further categorized into four categories:

❑ Personal—a review of highly personal and unique wants and needs that only the individuals can discuss and decide.

❑ Psychological—a focus on inner feelings and concerns about life after retirement and the need to establish goals.

❑ Physiological—the need to develop specific programs to address physical and mental conditioning.

❑ Practical—a practical appraisal of lifestyle and what you want to do in retirement, concluding with the need to plan beyond your life and finally to integrate your financial plan into your retirement plan.

The chart on the next page lists the ten steps that are explained in detail in the book. The message is that if you work through each of the ten steps with your spouse or partner, you will have a really good foundation upon which to start your retirement experience. Plus, the process of discussing the issues within each step will create a new sense of anticipation, excitement and purpose for the years ahead.

Personalized Retirement Plan (PRP)

Personal

1. Identify and distinguish between what you **want** to do and what you **need** to do in retirement.
2. Determine the **obligations and commitments** that influence your retirement planning.
3. Conduct a **personal inventory** strengths, weaknesses, opportunities and threats.

Psychological

4. Learn how to adjust to **Life after Retirement.**
5. Validate your **goals in life.**

Physiological

6. Maintain or improve your **physical conditioning.**
7. Maintain your **mental conditioning.**

Practical

8. Determine your preferences for **lifestyle, location and leisure** activities.
9. Develop your **"exit strategy".**
10. Integrate your **financial plan** into your overall retirement plan.

At the end of each planning step is a series of key questions that summarize the most important discussion points. When you fill in your responses to the key questions, the final responses will be the outline for your own Personalized Retirement Plan; a plan that covers all aspects of your retirement journey.

The third section, **Insights and Words of Wisdom,** is a series of observations gleaned from discussions with current retirees about things that they think are important about retirement planning or things that new retirees need to consider and keep in top of mind.

The epilog is an introspective review of the things the author learned in writing the book and is intended to serve as a reminder and motivator of the issues that are vital for effective retirement planning.

Finally, the last chapter in the book introduces a concept called the *Wisdom Corps.* Similar to the Peace Corps, the Wisdom Corps identifies what may well be the greatest asset of our time; namely, the under-utilized experience and wisdom in the minds of retirees around the world. If we, as a global society, can find a way to tap into this resource, it could well become the greatest opportunity in the history of mankind.

Section One

A New Look at Retirement Planning

A Perspective about Retirement...

"When one door closes, another one opens but we often look so long and regretfully at the closed door that we fail to see the one that has opened for us."

~Alexander Graham Bell

Chapter 1

Retirement Renaissance
An Overview

"It takes a lot of courage to release the familiar and seemingly secure, to embrace the new. But there is no real security in what is no longer meaningful. There is more security in the adventurous and exciting, for in movement there is life, and in change there is power."
~Alan Cohen, Author

The historical *Renaissance* of the 14th century was a transition of the world from medieval to modern times and ushered in three centuries of cultural renewal, change, resurgence and awakening. There is a *renaissance* beginning to occur in the way Baby Boomers think about and plan for retirement. The expectation of a "gold watch at 65" or a traditional retirement is changing. The Boomers are challenging the existing paradigm about when to retire, what to do in retirement, or whether to retire at all in a traditional sense. Many Boomers will continue to work, full or part-time; regardless of their economic status because they view work and career as an integral part of a whole and satisfying lifestyle. The new paradigm views retirement as one possible option rather than a necessity. *Retirement Renaissance* explains the phenomenon and how it will impact your retirement plans. The key message is that you need more than a financial plan to navigate the new world of retirement planning.

At the center of the renaissance is the change in the attitude about the purpose and role of work and retirement in one's life. The purpose of work is tied directly to economic survival. We are motivated to work in order to earn money to survive. If the motivation to work was purely economic, man would be no better than a machine. But man seeks a higher purpose, that's where the role of work comes into play. The role or nature of work can provide the worker with a sense of accomplishment and personal satisfaction. If a person really enjoys his or her work, then they will do it better and receive more enjoyment and satisfaction from the experience.

In earlier times people were less concerned about personal satisfaction than they were about the practical necessity to earn a living. Although many skilled laborers experienced high levels of personal fulfillment, many in the working class viewed work simply as a necessary requirement. In this light, it was easy for work to become dull, boring and somewhat impersonal. It is sad but true that some people may have worked an entire career at a job they didn't like and received little enjoyment from, but did it out of necessity.

I remember an incident in the summer after I graduated from high school. I was undecided if I would go to college so I got a job working on an assembly line in a large manufacturing plant. I was making more money as a novice worker than I had ever seen before in my life. All my previous part-time jobs were minimum wage. The man next to me on the assembly line had worked in the same plant, on the same line, doing the same job, making the same product for 32 years. It was a boring job. I asked him one day how he was able to keep a positive attitude and he responded, "Well, son, it's all about making a living. I got seniority. I will retire in three years with a company pension and then I will kiss this blankety-blank place goodbye forever!" We had more talks during the summer and it became apparent that although he was financially secure, he wasn't happy with the way his career turned out. He had stopped dreaming and settled into accumulating seniority. Our conversations made me reconsider my personal career options and at the end of the summer, I left the assembly line and enrolled in college. I was the first person in my family to advance beyond high school. My experience on the assembly line provided the motivation to enroll in college and position myself for a broader range of career opportunities. The bottom line is that I didn't want to regret several decades later that I had not explored additional learning opportunities.

One has to wonder how many workers there are like my friend on the assembly line. For people who put in their time solely to make a living, there has to be an inner sadness about their career that welcomes the idea of retirement. Retirement for them is a reward or a goal to reach after several decades of hard, perhaps ungratifying work. It is no wonder that some people count down the years and months and days until they can finally retire and get on with doing things that they really want to do.

The History of Retirement

The concept of retirement did not become a cultural expectation until after World War II. Prior generations worked until they were no longer physically able. There were few pension programs or retirement savings plans. The post Industrial Revolution era ushered in the division of labor and assembly lines. The result was the creation of many non-skilled jobs that were dull and boring, certainly not challenging or personally fulfilling. There is no intent to demean the contribution of the millions of blue-collar workers who helped to build this great country. The point is that the Industrial Revolution created many types of jobs that were routine, boring and failed to maximize a person's mental capability.

In the past, individual craftsmen made an entire product from scratch with their own hands. The products that came from the new factories and assembly lines were produced by dozens or hundreds of people. The consequence was the difficulty for individuals to develop a personal sense of accomplishment or satisfaction for doing only a small part of the process. It is not surprising that some workers were delighted to have the opportunity to retire with a pension. Eventually, retirement programs became the norm and people worked their 30 or 40 years and retired. It was assumed that retirement would be a time of happiness, rest and relaxation. That was the expectation.

When the dust settled, there were a lot of workers with pent up frustration about their job and career. The sons and daughters of these retirees, the Baby Boomers, lived through their parent's experiences with work and retirement. There is strong evidence to suggest that if a Boomer was raised in a home where their parents went to work out of a sense of obligation rather than personal satisfaction, their sons and daughters were highly motivated to pursue a career path that provided the opportunity to achieve higher levels of personal satisfaction and fulfillment. That is why the Boomers embarked en masse into careers in the professions: law, medicine, science, education and technology. A far lesser number followed in their parents' footsteps and worked at a job to simply make a living and eventually retire.

There are many Baby Boomers that were the first person in their family to go to college. The Boomers became the most educated generation ever and translated their education into the creation of the greatest economic boom in the history of the world.

The age of the retiring Baby Boomer is now at hand. For the most part, they view work, career and retirement in a more positive vein. If a Boomer has worked in a job that they truly enjoy, it is quite possible they will question whether or not they should consider a normal type of retirement. After all, why give up something that provides enjoyment, satisfaction and continuing financial rewards?

A new retirement paradigm is emerging. The paradigm has three characteristics: first, it is driven by the attitudes and feelings of Boomers who enjoy their work and career and don't necessarily see a need to retire; second, the newest retirement generation is living longer, they are healthier and more active, as a result, some will outlive their financial resources; third, the current economic crisis has contributed by shrinking the retirement nest eggs of many families and triggered the need to reevaluate or postpone retirement plans.

The result of this paradigm shift or Retirement Renaissance is that retirement will be viewed by many Boomers more as a lifestyle decision than an expected requirement. There will be some Boomers who will retire much like their parents and grandparents. But there will also be a significant number who will retire a day at a time, or continue to work until they no longer add value, or the work is no longer enjoyable, or work part-time at the current job, or retire and go back to work in a new job or career of interest.

Key Point: The decision about when or whether to retire or what to do in retirement will be a personal, flexible option influenced by a person's attitudes and feelings and their economic and personal situation.

There is an important reality at play in the new Retirement Renaissance. If a person is blessed with having a job that they really enjoy, they never have to worry about how long they work, or what they have to do, or when they have to be at work, or coping with all the political issues in a typical work environment. They don't view their job as a separate activity that they work at eight or ten hours a day. They don't anxiously count down the hours every day, especially on Friday when they can begin to do things that they really enjoy. They don't daydream about retirement and count the years and months and days until retirement. For these pioneering retirement reformers, work is an integral part of their existence. They could no more remove work from their life than they could remove a vital organ from their bodies.

A new retirement paradigm is evolving. It suggests a synergistic harmony between all of the things that comprise a person's life; the relationship with their spouse, partner, family, community, church, social or leisure activities, and work itself. It is one integrated continuum of activity that defines their life and lifestyle. Therefore, they can't retire from work because it is an integral part of their being.

Guidelines for When to Retire

Of course, all things must eventually come to an end, including your career and job. There are three guidelines for determining when you should retire:

1. You are no longer having any fun.
2. You are no longer able to operate at the maximum level of skill and value.
3. You no longer have the same intense desire to jump out of bed and go to work.

If any of these symptoms occur in your life, then you know it's time to hang it up. Until then, enjoy your career and life to the fullest. Don't be like some professional ball players who try to play beyond their prime and end up sullying their previous hard earned and deserving reputation. Work should be fun and exciting. When you lose your zest or slow down, even a tad, then you need to evaluate your future. The true story below illustrates the principle that when your job is no longer any fun, it is time to get out.

A True Story

Early in my career I bought a plaque during my travels entitled, *"The 10 Commandments of Good Business Practice"*. The ten principles dealt with issues like honesty, integrity, hard work, commitment, loyalty, empathy, etc. The plaque hung on my office wall for about 15 years. Although I didn't look at it often, it was there as a reminder to practice the noble principles. The last commandment was unusual, it stated, "And, when it is no longer FUN, get out!" Eventually, the business was acquired and I went to work for the new company. We had many new problems and I grew frustrated with the bureaucracy of a much larger company. One day the CEO made a decision that I knew was wrong, but he was adamant that we implement the decision. I walked into my office in a foul mood, threw down my note pad and accidentally knocked a treasured vase off a shelf, it fell and broke. In a fit of rage, I whirled around and kicked the wall, hard. I felt something go "crunch" and limped off to the emergency room with a broken foot. While recuperating, I hobbled into my office and suddenly took note of the 10 commandments plaque. The last commandment suddenly lit up in my mind like a neon sign, "…when it is no longer FUN, get out!" I realized that I had been terribly unhappy for a long time but I hung in there for lots of reasons, many having to do with loyalty. I sat there pensively and made a life-changing decision. Then I wrote my letter of resignation and gave it to my boss. Suddenly I felt as if a great weight had been lifted from my shoulders. I had no idea what I was going to do next, but I felt good about the decision. My work was no longer any fun, so I got out.

If you are planning to retire, or are already retired, and you have had thoughts about the purpose and role of work in your life, take comfort in the fact that there are lots of people just like you who still enjoy their work and careers and don't see any reason why they should retire completely or abruptly from their committed lifestyle.

Chapter 2

The Changing World of Retirement Planning

"They must often change, who would be constant in happiness or wisdom."
                                                                    ~Confucius

The world of retirement planning is changing rapidly. As more and more seniors approach retirement, some are beginning to question the concept of a traditional retirement, especially those who are still enjoying their job and career. This chapter will expand on several issues and trends that are changing the way seniors think about and plan for retirement. The changes cannot be ignored because they are real and present. Every new or retired senior will have to adjust their retirement plans to accommodate these changes.

❑ **Impact of the Global Economic Recession**—the impact of the global economic recession has created a retirement crisis for many potential retirees. The sudden decrease in the size of retirement portfolios is causing many seniors to delay their retirement plans or possibly eliminate the dream of a traditional retirement. Many seniors will continue their careers or work part-time to supplement their retirement income. The wealthiest seniors who have ample retirement funds will be in a minority of eligible retirees. The impact of the global recession will be visible for many years to come as seniors adjust their careers and lifestyles to accommodate the financial realities.

Although the financial crisis is an unexpected problem, it also presents an opportunity in disguise. A great many corporations and institutions will benefit significantly by having some of their most experienced people continue working in key roles. The experience and wisdom of the senior workers should result in more productivity and the opportunity to provide a well-planned mentoring and knowledge transfer to the next generation.

In addition, healthcare costs have increased at an unprecedented level. Many retirees have not planned adequately or created a large enough retirement fund to offset healthcare costs and their own life expectancy. They now find themselves in a real or potential financial crisis.

For those new retirees or soon-to-be retirees, the recent economic and political dynamics add an additional dimension to the planning process. Many retirees will have to rethink their previous positions on retirement goals due to the impact of the global financial crisis.

The benefit in the midst of crisis may well be the realization that retirement planning is now more of a necessity than it might have previously been. The crisis has gotten everyone's attention and may lead to a more introspective and deeper level of retirement planning. Whatever position a retiree may now be in, the information in this book will provide a planning tool to use in steering a course through these turbulent times.

You must review your financial plan with a trained financial advisor to ensure that you have adequate retirement funds and that they are invested appropriately. If there is a shortfall, then you have a need to supplement your income by continuing to work, full or part-time.

Key Point: You have to deal with the reality of your particular situation and develop a plan for providing the additional financial resources if needed. Also, there should be no blame attached to a person's financial condition because lots of people are in the same boat, just deal with it and move on. The truth is that many retirees will benefit greatly from the need to get back to work, both financially and psychologically.

❑ **Influence of the Baby Boomers**—there are some 78 million Baby Boomers who are entering their retirement years over the next two decades. These new retirees are much different than their parents and grandparents. They are younger, more active, and healthier, have a longer life expectancy, and are much more adventuresome than prior generations. The combined attitudes and lifestyles of the new age retirees are creating a whole new way of thinking about and planning for the golden years of life. The concept of a traditional retirement will change significantly as people live longer, work longer, incorporate work into an integrated lifestyle, or explore new and different ways to achieve happiness and personal fulfillment.

When most retirees started their careers, it was assumed that a traditional kind of retirement was the desired goal. The traditional retirement planning paradigm was based on certain assumptions about one's physical and financial condition, specifically life expectancy and financial resources. With retirees living longer and expenses rising faster than anticipated, many seniors have already or will soon deplete their retirement nest egg. The options include a return to work, either full or part-time, if physically capable, or reliance on financial assistance from children or social welfare sources.

There are also many seniors who want to delay or postpone retirement because they are not yet ready to retire. The fact is that seniors are healthier and more active. The average 65 year old retiree is a much different physical specimen than his or her father, mother or grandparents. As a result, many potential retirees look younger, act younger and are not ready to rest and relax at the normal retirement age.

A great many potential retirees are opting to continue in their careers, either full or part-time, because they enjoy what they are doing. You can think of this new breed of retiree as a retirement pioneer. They will call their own shots as to when they retire, if ever, in a traditional sense.

❑ **New Retirement Paradigm**—the economic environment has accelerated and brought into focus another trend involving a transformation or *renaissance* that is beginning to occur with the basic premise of a traditional retirement. The expectation of a "gold watch at 65" is rapidly changing because of the mindset of the Baby Boomers. The new generation is challenging the existing paradigm about when to retire, what to do in retirement, or whether to retire at all in a traditional sense. Many Boomers will continue to work, full or part-time; regardless of their economic status because they view their work and career as an integral part of a whole and satisfying lifestyle. Work and life are synonymous. As a result, a new retirement paradigm is beginning to emerge. The new paradigm views retirement as one possible option rather than a necessity.

It is highly probable that the Baby Boomers will change the thought process about retirement and challenge the existing norms and traditions. The new retirees will also be more outspoken about what they prefer to do in retirement as opposed to doing what other generations might expect of them. As a result, it is likely that the Baby Boomers will continue to be a vital contributing force in our society.

These retirement pioneers will eventually create a new post-career paradigm that allows them to allocate more time to things that they enjoy doing, whether it is work or family or recreation or church or community. But, significantly, work will always be an integral part of the retirement lifestyle of a great many future retirees.

Key Point: Retirement planning will become a personalized, individual option rather than a "one size fits all" requirement. The new retirement paradigm will cause many of the Baby Boomers to re-evaluate their retirement options based more on personal preference and need than on societal expectations. It is possible that the children and grandchildren of the Baby Boomers, the Generation X'ers and Y'ers, will cause the retirement paradigm to shift even further as they re-define the intrinsic relationship between work, technology and the whole life experience.

It is certainly possible that traditional retirement may become a thing of the past as more and more potential retirees integrate their lifestyles with their career, family, leisure time activities, personal goals and desires. In this new integrated lifestyle model, there would be no need to retire because a person's career would become an inseparable part of one's personal framework. As a society we would evolve back to a condition that existed centuries ago where craftsmen and skilled tradesmen worked their entire lives, with no thought of retiring, to perfect their skills for both personal and financial benefit.

The newest generation of retirees, the Baby Boomers, will reshape the traditional view of retirement. The previous retirement paradigm was fashioned by the Greatest Generation of the 1920s and the Silent Generation of the 1930s. These generations were characterized by a strong work ethic that was tempered by the Great Depression. They viewed work as a requirement and obligation.

After the economic prosperity of post World War II, many in these generations were afforded an opportunity to retire with pensions and Social Security benefits, something that many of their fathers and mothers never received. As a result, the concept of retirement was gradually accepted as the norm with millions of blue-collar workers and professionals retiring at age 65 or earlier. A healthy Social Security System enhanced the probability of retirement. As a result, many of these retirees simply dropped out of the workforce and wiled away their time with no particular plans other than to rest and relax. Eventually retirement became a desired, sought after benefit and the traditional retirement paradigm was accepted by society.

The benefit of retirement is that it provided the retiree with a well-deserved reward for a career of hard work and productivity. The irony of retirement is that a person's mental and physical skills are put on the shelf when their experience and wisdom are at their highest. Also ironically, the American and European cultures no longer place their elders in a position of rank and respect. Instead of using the collective experience and wisdom of the senior population, the contemporary cultures put them out to pasture. Historically other cultures revered their elders and used their collective wisdom for the benefit of the entire community.

There was an enormous loss of talent and wisdom from these generations of men and women who helped to shape the destiny of the world during and after World War II. Our nation would have been wise to use the experience and wisdom of these prior generations to mentor and counsel the next generation. The lesson to be learned is that there is a significant place in society for the "elders of the tribe" who can contribute mightily to society in general if they are afforded the opportunity to be a part of the decision-making process.

If previous generations saw a clear line between work and personal life, it is possible that future generations will view work and personal life as one integrated continuum, therefore no need for something called retirement. But, that is in the future, for now we are experiencing a new emerging paradigm about traditional retirement practices.

The Facts About Retirement

The fact is that more and more retirees are continuing to work or are going back to work because they can't afford to retire comfortably or they outlived their retirement resources. From a recent AARP publication, "The Bureau of Labor Statistics (BLS) reports that between 2000 and 2008, the number of workers aged 65 to 69 rose 25%. Even greater increases were cited for those ages 70 to 74 (32%), ages 75 to 79 (38%) and 80 and over (67%). The bottom line is that, as people live longer, public expectations with retirement are in "a period of transition". Given the demographic changes afoot...this evolution in attitudes is likely to continue for years to come." So there it is, the retirement paradigm is changing and it probably won't be much different for the Baby Boomers. Continuing the quote, "According to the Center for Retirement Research at Boston College, 52% of boomers born between 1948 and 1954 are at risk for being unable to maintain their standard of living in retirement. And it will get worse: 64% of boomers born between 1955 and 1964 and 72% of Gen X-ers born between 1964 and 1974 may be unable to retire comfortably in their lifetime." The overriding conclusion is that most retirees do not have an adequate nest egg to survive if retirement lasts for 20 or more years. There is also another powerful change occurring with retirement planning; namely, the nature of work is changing and a great many potential retirees will continue to work simply because they love their jobs and career. They have been able to integrate work into a personal lifestyle that allows them the freedom to explore other interests and activities without giving up their job or way of living. The net result is that this will no longer be "your father's Oldsmobile" when it comes to planning for retirement.

❑ **Technology and the Nature of Work**—the Boomers are technologically savvy. They are the first generation to fully embrace technology and make use of the extraordinary capabilities to bring about dramatic improvement in the way work is performed. As a result, the nature of work is changing as people use technology to make work easier, more productive, and less dependent upon being at the "plant" or "office". It is reasonable to expect that many types of jobs could be conducted away from the traditional workplace, whether it is an office, plant, classroom, store, etc. As more work is changed by technology, the whole concept of "going to work" will change and allow people to integrate their work into a personal lifestyle that blends all aspects of their life: work, spouse, family, and community, church, and leisure activities. Some types of jobs will allow people to monitor work results while involved in other activities. In this scenario, the need to "retire" will take on a different meaning because the work routine or process will allow the individual to multi-task and perform work and other activities simultaneously. Some careers and jobs will make it easier for people to "retire" into a more leisurely work environment and possibly extend the need to retire in a conventional sense.

Prior generations worked with their hands to produce products. The majority of the workers today are involved in service industries. Where before there were larger numbers of blue collar workers, currently there is a majority of white collar and pink collar workers. Where previously the worker had to be physically present in the plant, factory, or office, today it is possible for large numbers of workers to work wherever and whenever they desire.

As a result of the new retirement paradigm, there will be more and more of a new category of worker, the "gray" collar; a senior who continues to work or returns to work. The gray collar worker represents a tremendous opportunity for the corporate and professional world to utilize the experience and wisdom to help transform companies and industries.

Technology has played a major role in the transition to a vast service economy. The majority of the workers today are involved in service industries that utilize a full range of human skills and intelligence. The worldwide economy is transitioning into an interdependent society with supply and demand being influenced by global rather than purely national influences. The children and grandchildren of the Boomers, the X and Y generations will further utilize technology to create yet unknown and spectacular changes in the way people work and communicate.

As the lines blur between work and personal life, so too will there be a re-definition of benefits like vacation and retirement. In essence, workers will be more independent than ever before and capable of managing their time and output on their schedule. The net result might well be that workers will develop a skill or trade and continue doing it their entire career as an integrated part of their whole life experience. If this sounds familiar, it is the way life was in the pre-Industrial Revolution era where craftsmen worked their entire career at their specialty without the need to retire.

❑ **Financial Planning vs. Retirement Planning**—another issue that impacts the new view of retirement planning is that most existing retirement plans are not actually retirement plans at all, they are essentially financial plans; and, most books on retirement planning deal almost exclusively with financial planning, not retirement planning. Although the two terms, financial planning and retirement planning, are used interchangeably, there is a fundamental difference. Financial planning is a component of a comprehensive retirement plan. The assumption is that if a retiree has enough money to live happily ever after, everything else will fall in place. The experience of veteran retirees suggests that this singular focus on financial planning is incomplete. Although financial planning is a vital requirement for a secure retirement, it is only one important consideration.

The traditional retirement planning process has historically been based on financial planning. As a result, many earlier generations of retirees failed to consider a more in-depth retirement planning process that addressed all the personal and practical issues that retirees deal with on a day-to-day basis. *Retirement Renaissance* provides a blueprint for creating a full and complete retirement plan.

The new retirees perceive retirement as an opportunity to maximize their whole life experience by integrating work, family and leisure activities into one well-rounded and satisfying experience. This view recognizes the need to plan all aspects of retirement to ensure a satisfying whole life experience. It is hoped that eventually the financial planners of the world will realize that retirement planning involves more than money. *Retirement Renaissance* positions financial planning as an important, integrated component of retirement planning, not the only component.

The goal of *Retirement Renaissance* is to provide the retiree or soon-to-be-retired senior, and the spouse or partner, with the tools and techniques needed to plan all aspects of retirement. The message is simple; the better prepared you are for all aspects of retirement, the better you will be able to deal with the challenges and opportunities.

□ **Potential Insolvency of the Social Security System**—the Social Security System reserves are under enormous stress due to larger numbers of retirees, both the Baby Boomers and the influx of eligible immigrants. People are living longer and taking more money out of the system. The percentage of wage earners contributing to the system and the percent of contributions has declined due to layoffs, company closings, offshore outsourcing, and the overall impact of the economic crisis.

It is a rather sobering statistic that the <u>average</u> retiree today does not have enough of a financial nest egg to last throughout their retirement and life expectancy. In fact, many financial retirement plans were developed several decades ago when the mortality tables were much shorter than present.

For instance, according to the most recent statistics from the Center for Disease Control, the average life expectancy for a person at birth is 77.8 years for males and 80.4 years for females. If a person retires at the traditional age of 65, they will need to provide 12 to 15 years of coverage. However, if a person lives to age 65, their life expectancy after 65 increases to 18.7 years for males and 20.0 years for females, or 83.7 years for males and 87.8 years for females. How many retirees have created financial resources to provide 18 to 20 years of financial resources, or more, at their desired level of living with adequate reserves to handle medical or other emergencies? Not many retirees are so fortunate.

How Big is Your Retirement Nest Egg?

How much of a nest egg do you need to retire comfortably without worrying about money? The answer is that it all depends on your lifestyle and budget. For instance, some people can get by comfortably on $3000 a month while some people require $30,000 a month. Let's say you need only $3000 a month or $36,000 a year. If you and your partner live for 20 years after you retire, with no additional income, you will need a nest egg of $720,000 ($36,000 x 20 = $720,000). These are approximate numbers and do not consider investment growth, inflation or any other significant expense issue that might drain financial resources.

If the Social Security System in the United States goes bankrupt or dramatically reduces monthly benefits, there will be an even greater number of retirees who will have to extend their working careers due to financial necessity.

If there is no meaningful Social Security or private retirement funds, the consequence will be monumental to the viability and financial well-being of a large number of senior citizens. In addition, there will be an immeasurable impact on the social welfare systems of the federal, state and local governments.

Key Point: If you do not have adequate financial resources to protect your desired lifestyle over your life expectancy, above and beyond Social Security, it would be a good idea to delay a traditional retirement and work full or part-time to add to your retirement nest egg. You will also need to ensure that your current retirement funds are invested wisely. You should contact a professional financial planner and ask for assistance.

Summary—there is a Retirement Renaissance taking place. Some might call it a retirement "revolution" because the Boomers will have a sudden and dramatic impact on today's global culture. There will be new challenges, for instance:

❑ The economic and social impact of having more senior workers in all types of jobs.
❑ The impact on corporate policies, practices and work rules that will be altered or eliminated to accommodate an aging workforce.
❑ The financial impact on existing pensions and benefit programs.
❑ The impact on families who will care for aging parents and grandparents.
❑ The dramatic impact the Boomers will have on the health and social welfare systems as they live longer and avail themselves of the existing resources.

But there will also be new opportunities. Think about the potential benefits that will accrue to the economy from a productive, dependable, proven senior workforce. Perhaps the biggest and best opportunity is the potential for utilizing the experience and wisdom of the expanding senior population to address challenges in education, government and the corporate world. This talent resource represents perhaps the greatest potential asset in our country's human treasury.

We are living in a dynamic and challenging era.

Chapter 3

Retirement Redefined

"Retirement has been a discovery of beauty for me. I never had the time before to notice the beauty of my grandkids, my wife, and the tree outside my very own front door. And, the beauty of time itself."
~Hartman Jule

Let's take a closer look at the word "retirement." The dictionary defines retirement as the *"act of removing oneself from the daily routine of work."* Another interpretation is *"to depart for rest."* When we talk about retirement, we tend not to think about the literal interpretation of the word. We are more apt to think about a generalized attitude or perception that retirement implies a new phase of our life in which we slow down, rest, take it easy, and engage in enjoyable activities. The internalized perception that most people have of retirement is that it is more of a departure from certain activities than a commencement of a new experience.

All of us dreamed about retirement during our career, especially on those cold, dreary mornings when the alarm clock went off at 5:30am and we pulled ourselves out of bed and trudged to work through a foot of snow. When we could hardly bear it any longer, we allowed our mind to wander into the imaginary world of retirement and we saw ourselves walking on a tropical beach, kicking at sea shells and wondering what we might want to do the rest of the day, if anything. Then we were jolted back to reality when he got to our job and faced the real world. But we took comfort in counting down the years, months, weeks, and days to retirement.

Retirement was a goal that kept us going during the difficult times. We used retirement as an incentive to hang in there and persevere until the bitter end. Eventually the final day of work comes and we suddenly get launched into retirement. The last day of work is a bittersweet experience. On one hand it is one of the happiest days of one's life. There are parties and gifts and tremendous camaraderie. On the other hand it is a really sad and emotionally difficult day. It isn't easy to leave good friends and colleagues.

The next day, or the first day of retirement, begins the initiation ritual of retirement, unless you postpone the inevitable by leaving on a world cruise. Whether immediately or eventually, there will come a day early in your retirement when you wake up, look at that fifty or sixty year old body in the mirror and say, "Now what?"

Unless you have developed a fairly rigid program of activities, you may not know what to do with yourself, literally. For instance, one of my close friends retired and within a week his wife was ready to have him go back to work. It seems that he wanted to help her around the house more than she wanted or needed his help. In desperation she exclaimed, "For God's sake, go back to work! I have somehow managed to run this house for the past 35 years. What in the world makes you suddenly think that I need your help?" My friend was mystified by his wife's reaction. All he wanted to do was help.

Another friend yearned for years to be retired so he could spend more time playing golf. After a month of hanging out at the golf club, he realized that he really didn't want to play golf every day. Clearly his expectations of retirement did not match up with the reality of his experience.

There are lots of other examples of people who retire and begin to experience some second thoughts about the intent and purpose of retirement.

I think a part of the problem has to do with the word itself, "*retirement.*" My contention is that if you simply stop working and don't replace this activity with some other meaningful activity, you may experience some degree of discontent or depression and run the risk of missing out on one of the greatest opportunities of your life. The Golden Years are supposed to be a time of great satisfaction and happiness. But the key to success is to focus on "starting" new things rather than "stopping" old and traditional things.

A Better Name for Retirement?

I think we should consider a better name for retirement. The new name should imply the beginning of a new and rewarding part of one's life. For instance, when young people graduate from high school or college the ceremony is called a "commencement." The implication of the word is right on target, not graduation or the end of something but the start of a new and exciting part of their lives.

Perhaps a more appropriate name for retirement might be the "*renaissance years.*" Renaissance implies a *new beginning,* a rebirth, revitalization, regeneration, and a new start on the rest of a person's life. What better way to think about retirement than to seek a personal renaissance that brings about significant change and opportunity in the latter stages of a person's life. All of that is possible if you consider that retirement is a new beginning rather than the end of something. Retirement could be referred to as the "renaissance years."

I believe the difference between the words, retirement and renaissance, is more than semantics. It is a mindset that can create a positive and adventurous attitude about the future rather than an inward focus on all the things that one will miss about their career.

Most people identify the word retirement with the absence of any meaningful work. The assumption is that the retiree will cease working and spend their time relaxing and taking it easy. From a psychological point of view, the retiree who sees retirement as a time to get away from work is more likely to wile away their time and talent than the person who views retirement as simply another opportunity to achieve something.

If we used "renaissance years" rather than retirement, it might cause us to view the Golden Years as just another opportunity to realize the next goal. It puts a more positive spin on retirement and opens the door to the exploration of lots of exciting options.

But regardless of what we call it, there are lots of people who have a difficult time adjusting to the total impact of retirement. It is my hope that this book will provide the tools to use, whether you are enjoying retirement or experiencing problems, to help you get more out of your retirement years than perhaps you had ever imagined.

A Look into the Future of Retirement

Most new retirees will live longer and have the potential to enjoy the fruits of retirement for far more years than prior generations.

A great many of the new retirees will either delay their retirement or retire and go back to work because some retirees will not be ready to retire. If you believe you are at the top of your game and you want to continue working, or you have a need to maintain a certain standard of living, then it is perfectly okay to postpone retirement, or evolve into a condition of permanent non-retirement.

One solution might be to simply continue working, which some will do, either because of financial necessity or personal preference. Another option might be to create programs that encourage desiring seniors to continue working in a scaled down capacity while providing the employer with the opportunity to download the essence of experience and wisdom to the next generation of workers. But if this concept is to be successful, the business leaders and politicians will have to step in and create new guidelines and laws for retirement.

Age alone should not be the predominant factor in determining retirement. Ponder the quote by Bernard Baruch...

"Age is only a number, a cipher for the records. A man can't retire his experience. He must use it."

It is ironic but many people retire when they are literally at the peak of their experience and wisdom. All of this experience and wisdom runs the risk of going down the drain unless the individual can find a way to use it or the corporations and institutions of the world wake up and realize that they must find a way to preserve and use this enormous resource.

Granted, some seniors may have rushed out the door to retirement when it was slightly ajar, but there are many others who would have preferred to work, in some capacity, to utilize the investment that they made in developing their skills and capabilities. Plus, there are lots of people who simply like to work. Some will prefer to work part-time in some capacity during retirement.

We are living in an age of a Retirement Renaissance. If you want to realize your full potential, you need to develop your personal PRP and determine what you want to do to with the rest of your life and career.

Chapter 4

Purpose of Retirement

"Who knows what we live, and struggle, and die for? Wise men write many books, in words too hard to understand. But this, the purpose of our lives, the end of all our struggle, is beyond all human wisdom. "
~Alan Paton, Humanist

If someone posed the question, "W*hat is the purpose of retirement?*" How would you respond? We don't tend to think about retirement as having a purpose like we would about our education or career or family. Most people would probably respond and say that the purpose of retirement is to rest and relax after a long career or that retirement will be a time when you don't have to be responsible for anything, other than taking it easy and enjoying life.

But it doesn't always work out like that. Retirement is like any other important phase of life; you will get out of it what you plan to get out of it. If you establish a purpose for retirement, you can then work toward achieving your purpose.

When you stop to think about it, every phase of your life has a purpose. The purpose of going to school is to become educated. The purpose of marriage is to have a spouse and family. The purpose of your career is to develop a trade or profession that allows you to provide for your family and achieve success at what you do. Yet some people fail to grasp the notion that retirement should have a purpose.

For instance, one example of a purpose in retirement is to achieve personal fulfillment. If you had this kind of purpose, you would devote yourself to identifying and working on those things that represent fulfillment for you.

Another purpose might be to explore a totally new career like learning to become an accomplished chef or opening a bed and breakfast inn or becoming a published author or devoting yourself to volunteer work.

Perhaps the most common purpose for retirement might be simply to rest and relax. This purpose implies that you will seek a life of leisure with an emphasis on simply taking it easy. There is nothing wrong with that. The important point is that you predetermined that rest and relaxation was your primary purpose.

Your retirement purpose is personal and will not be the same for everyone. The key is to make sure that you establish a purpose. If not, there is a good chance that you might wander through the early years of retirement hoping to find something that makes you happy, sort of like going through a buffet hoping you will find something you like.

There is another way to look at it. Ask yourself the question, "If retirement doesn't have a purpose, then why do we bother to retire?" There has got to be a purpose for why you retire other than you are old enough and have enough money.

It might be helpful to establish a better perspective and understanding about how the concept of retirement came into being so you can see why retirement should have a purpose.

Retirement in Perspective

Earlier we discussed the fact that retirement is a fairly recent invention. The workers in the 1800s and early 1900s didn't retire. They worked as long as they were physically able. There were not a great many retirement and pension plans in the industrialized countries. In the United States, the Social Security Act was enacted in August 1935 and provided a foundation for retirement planning. Retirement did not become a part of our traditions until after World War II. The boom years following the Great War also ushered in a new era of industrial relations and unionization that resulted in the introduction of retirement and pension plans for millions of blue and white collar workers. Eventually, retirement became an accepted and desirable practice. For the past 60 or so years, retirement has been the expected norm and expectation for the end of a person's career.

The upside of retirement has always been the opportunity for a person to spend quality time doing whatever pleases them in their retirement years. However, some retirees also experienced depression and melancholy when they failed to realize how important a person's job and identity was for their emotional well-being. If the retiree fails to compensate for the loss of their job and career with other meaningful activities, there is strong evidence to suggest that many retirees begin a slow and inevitable decline in their physical and mental capabilities.

Retirement should always have a purpose. At the end of the day if there are no goals or an end purpose for retirement, how does anyone know if their retirement will be successful? Retirement should not be the equivalent of an unplanned trip. Not too many people would drive across the country without first looking at a road map and developing an itinerary. So it is in retirement, if you don't have a purpose and plan, you won't know where you are going or how you are going to get there.

Once you agree on a purpose for retirement then you can begin to think about the *reason* behind why you want to pursue your retirement purpose. If you don't have a reason why you want to retire, then you might just as well continue doing what you're already doing.

I talked to a great many seniors and retirees and boiled down all of their comments into three overriding reasons why people decide to retire. See if any of these purposes make sense for you.

Why do people retire?
There are three reasons or motivations for why people retire.
1. Reward yourself for a successful career.
2. Transition from what you **need** to do to what you **want** to do the rest of your life.
3. Strive to achieve a sense of satisfaction and fulfillment for your life's experience.

Let's take a closer look at each motivation.

Reward Yourself for a Successful Career

Most of us work our entire careers with the ultimate goal of retiring. But when we get to retirement, some of us continue doing the same old, same old with the exception that we no longer go to work. One of the most important objectives of retirement is to *enjoy yourself, have fun, and do your thing.*

Retirement should be viewed as a reward for a successful career. You should celebrate retirement because you made it, not everyone does. Therefore, you want to enjoy life to the fullest for the rest of your life. Just relax and enjoy the newfound freedom. You should never feel bad about simply enjoying the fruits of your labor.

There are some of you who may not be able to enjoy retirement to its fullest simply because you will fail to decide what you really want to do that will make you happy. Or, you won't break away from the traditions and conservative tendencies of your past, especially when it comes to spending money for pure enjoyment.

If you find yourself wiling away your time with nothing in particular to do or engaging in meaningless activities while hoping against hope that something exciting will happen, all I can say is you need to reevaluate the purpose of your retirement before you fall into the ranks of the couch potatoes.

There is literally no excuse for not enjoying retirement. If you are experiencing some adjustment problems in retirement, you have the power to change your life. No one can help if you don't first recognize that you have a problem and then seek help. Don't waste another day dwelling on your retirement concerns; make the decision that the first purpose of retirement is to enjoy life to the fullest.

Transition from what you NEED to do to what you WANT to do

The first great opportunity you have in retirement is to do what you really want to do, not what you previously needed to do to make a living or fulfill a career objective or obligation. If you always dream of doing something that you really wanted to do, then retirement is the time to do it. A great many retirees will transition to a life of leisure and engage in pleasurable activities. Others may start down a predetermined path of leisure activities and eventually determine that they want to do something else. No problem, just make adjustments and pursue a new direction. The point is that retirement is your time to do what you really want to do. Note: You will read more about the differences between wants and needs in Chapter 9, Step One in the Personalized Retirement Plan.

For some retirees, the transition may be a continuance of what they were doing during their career, either because they like what they do, or they need the additional income. In other words, they want to continue what they were doing and perhaps eventually slow down or work on a part-time basis. There are lots of retirees who work part-time and play part-time.

Still others may opt to start a whole new career and delay the leisure time activities or incorporate them on a time-available basis. It is not uncommon for a professional person, like a dentist, to "retire" from their practice and go back to work full or part-time as a professor in a dental school to fulfill a lifelong ambition or simply because they want to start a new career. The important point is that they are doing what they want to do and retirement provides them with the opportunity to do what they want to do.

Strive to achieve a sense of satisfaction and fulfillment

The third reason for retirement is to strive to achieve a sense of satisfaction and fulfillment. Retirement provides an opportunity to assess one's life at the point of retirement and determine how satisfied you are with what you have accomplished. This is the ultimate form of self-reflection in which you review your life and give yourself a grade on your overall performance and results. If you can look yourself in the mirror and say, "I did okay", then you simply need to do whatever continues to make your happy in your retirement.

The key to personal evaluation should not be financial or how much money you were able to earn and sock away. There is much more to personal satisfaction that involves what you accomplished with your spouse and family, your profession, your church and community, your fellow man.

If you look at your overall accomplishments objectively and give yourself a mediocre or failing grade, then you need to use the later chapters in the book to determine what you need to do to achieve a sense of personal satisfaction and fulfillment. Remember that retirement represents the start of the last quarter of your life and there is a limited amount of time to get things squared away.

It doesn't matter what you did or plan to do, the important thing is how you feel about it. For instance, you can get a tremendous sense of satisfaction from painting your first amateurish watercolor or learning how to play the piano, but you can also feel really pleased with yourself for doing something that you have been putting off for weeks or months or years, like cleaning out a closet or washing the windows. The point is that things that bring about satisfaction don't have to be major tasks. You simply have to feel a sense of satisfaction from doing them.

There is one guideline that I have tried to follow: make sure you have at least one goal, one thing that you want to get done every single day. You can develop a long checklist of things to do but you will get satisfaction and feel good about yourself if you accomplish one thing a day.

A word of caution: there are times when you might cause more harm than good if you "force" yourself to enjoy something. For instance, if you play golf and you allow yourself to get angry or totally frustrated on the golf course, you may have to step back and remember that the purpose of the game is to have fun. If it isn't fun, or satisfying, then you should find something else to do that allows you to feel a sense of satisfaction.

Personal Fulfillment

The issue of fulfillment is a much bigger and more involved concept. Psychologists describe fulfillment or self-fulfillment as the final or ultimate goal in the striving to become a full and complete person.

After we satisfy our basic needs (food, clothing, shelter, safety, love, and esteem), we move toward achieving higher levels of need. The highest level of need or expectation is self-fulfillment or self-actualization. It is best described as "*the desire to become everything that one is capable of becoming.*" It is a condition in which a person strives to feel completely and totally satisfied with themselves and their accomplishments in life. It is unlikely that anyone will ever be totally satisfied because once you reach the goals you established to achieve fulfillment, things change and you pursue new goals.

Retirement represents an opportunity, in reality the last opportunity that you will have to accomplish the things that will bring about a sense of fulfillment. One way to describe the feeling is to imagine that you are taking your last breath and reflecting about everything that you have accomplished in your life. If you can honestly say that you are satisfied with what you have done, then you have achieved your personal goal of self-fulfillment and you are ready to find out what is behind the door to eternity.

If you place yourself in the present and ask the same question and you feel that there are still lots of things you have to do in order to develop a sense of accomplishment and fulfillment, then you need to start getting them done. The clock is ticking and you won't get a second chance.

The key to achieving self-fulfillment is not the recognition that you have achieved it; rather it is the striving for the goal that brings about an on-going feeling of satisfaction and accomplishment. But you have to first determine what it will take for you to develop a sense of self-fulfillment.

The *achievement of self-fulfillment should be the ultimate goal of a good life.* Enjoying life is great, but achieving a sense of fulfillment is the true purpose for our existence. Yet many of us fail to make plans for it to happen.

When a person is enjoying life, they are happy. When the enjoyment is constant and enduring, rather than temporary, it suggests that the person has found something that is rewarding and potentially fulfilling. For instance, those seniors who thought that they could find happiness by playing golf or tennis every day usually get bored. Most find that they need something more than a game or a single activity to keep them happy.

Common Characteristics of Happy Retirees

It is fairly easy to spot a happy retiree. They are the ones with a smile on their face and a pleasant disposition. From what I've observed, the retirees who are really enjoying their retirement have two things in common:

- *They are satisfied and content with **who they are and what they do.***
- *They **continue to learn and experience new challenges and opportunities** on their path to personal fulfillment.*

The two conditions of satisfaction and fulfillment work together. Satisfaction will lead to fulfillment when the joy or happiness is sustained. Usually this level of satisfaction comes from something more meaningful than a game or hobby.

For instance, one of my retired friends used to spend hours and hours on the tennis court after he retired. When he became bored, he got involved in his church and now spends a few days each week working with disadvantaged and handicapped children and adults. They take special-needs people to a golf driving range and teach them how to hit a golf ball. Although most of them are not very good at it, they are completely and totally enthralled by the experience. My friend leaves the range each day with a sense of satisfaction that few things in his corporate life or his days on the tennis court were able to match.

His new volunteer work helped him to advance his satisfaction into fulfillment because the new activity was far more rewarding. He hasn't abandoned tennis; he's simply added other activities to his schedule that took enjoyment to a higher level.

Fulfillment can come in many ways and at different times. It doesn't mean that you have to devote a significant amount of time helping other less fortunate people. It does, however, mean that the focus for fulfillment usually comes from outside yourself.

Key Point: You will always feel better when you do things for others rather than for yourself. That is the message for understanding the concept of fulfillment.

Secret to Achieving Fulfillment

Your challenge is to see if you can find what it will take for you and your partner to find happiness in retirement and ultimately achieve your own personal fulfillment.

There is no universal answer for what to do to achieve satisfaction and fulfillment. You have to learn how to adapt the principle to fit your particular situation. For instance, a retired surgeon may no longer have the nerves or vision to perform major surgeries. But he/she might achieve a high level of satisfaction and fulfillment from mentoring a younger surgeon on the psychological and personal side of being a successful surgeon.

An auto mechanic may not have the strength or contemporary skills to perform major engine repair. But he/she might be able to join a racing team as an advisor on the practical side of engine performance.

A management recruiter may have lost most of their prime networking contacts due to age and turnover. But he/she might be able to help smaller companies create a human resource function.

A teacher may have literally run out of steam from spending several decades in the front of the classroom. But he/she might get a tremendous sense of satisfaction from teaching English to new immigrants.

A nurse, like my wife, may shy away from the impact of technology in medical practice and the threat of unbridled liability, but she can conduct vision screening for pre-K kids to alert parents and teachers to potential vision problems (which she actually does and gains an untold level of satisfaction and fulfillment).

If you can use this book as a tool to help you figure out what you are good at doing and then can find an outlet for using that talent and experience, then it is highly likely that you will be able to gain a renewed level of satisfaction and fulfillment, whether you devote all or some of your time to the new found activity.

All you have to do is start the process to identify what you are good at and then find an outlet for your skills and capabilities. Your reward will be the potential for you to truly enjoy your retirement and hopefully achieve your own personal fulfillment. After all, that's what retirement and life is all about.

Chapter 5

The Post-Retirement Syndrome

"Try to relax and enjoy the crisis."
~Ashley Brilliant, Writer

There is an interesting malady that affects quite a few new retirees. The condition is triggered by the act of retiring and manifests itself in a level of despondency that runs from mild to severe. In mild cases of the affliction, the retiree may simply be somewhat dissatisfied or confused with the early stages of their retirement experience. For the more severely afflicted, the condition can bring about a serious depression and withdrawal from family and friends.

I can attest that this phenomenon is real because I experienced more than a mild case of this post-retirement malady. I researched the condition but was surprised that very little had been written about the plight of the newly retired. During my research, I recalled a similar type of depression that affects people in their 30s and 40s called the *mid-life or mid-career crisis.*

This mid-career crisis is a well-known phenomenon that has been studied and written about in great detail. Although psychologists recognize the mid-career crisis, they apparently have not yet turned their attention to the post-retirement malady. Since no one had yet named the post-retirement malady, I decided to call it the *post-retirement syndrome (PRS).* I was reluctant to call is a "crisis" because no one knows how extensive the condition may be or if it really is in the category of a crisis. All I can do is describe the condition and suggest that those who experience the symptoms are not alone and it is a normal reaction that affects a significant number of new retirees.

Each of these conditions could trigger a sense of loss, but the combination of all three can lead to the post-retirement syndrome. For many, the experience of actually retiring is similar to the trauma we all faced when we graduated from high school or college or started our first job or got married or had children and realized that a significant chapter in our lives had ended. It is not easy to adjust to significant change and many retirees are not prepared to cope with the negative impact of retirement.

In addition, all retirees eventually become much more aware of their own mortality because we all realize that we are now statistically closer to the end than the beginning. If these feelings are reinforced by an inner concern that something is missing, then we might experience some degree of emotional and psychological problems, or the *post-retirement syndrome.*

For all those who experienced mid-life crisis and would like to ignore or hide from the symptoms of PRS, all I can say is that this new phenomenon is real and must be faced with the same determination that was used to overcome the mid-life crisis.

If you are already retired and have experienced some significant adjustment issues, you might be experiencing the post-retirement syndrome. The good news is that it could represent a blessing in disguise because it will force you to come to grips with your inner self and resolve the issues that may have festered since your earlier life crisis. But this time around there is the acute awareness for all seniors that you no longer have the second half of your lives and careers to right the ship.

The reality of PRS is that the clock is ticking and there are only a limited number of years left to find true happiness and to achieve one's goals in life. If this book can serve as the motivation, then all you have to do is put your retirement plan into action.

Although much has been written about mid-life crisis, there is practically nothing written about problems that seniors experience in adjusting to retirement. It is possible that seniors who experience this malady might be walking in new snow and will have to blaze a new trail. It is also possible that the psychologists and counselors have not yet discovered the condition since many seniors who experience the condition don't want to talk about it because they are not willing to admit that they might have a problem. After all, retirement is supposed to be a time of great happiness, not a time of emotional and psychological upheaval.

In any event, the post-retirement syndrome is real and ultimately the medical and academic community will awaken to the need for action. It is also possible that this book could serve as the catalyst to bring about a greater awareness to the problem.

Symptoms of Post-Retirement Syndrome

"You might be a redneck if..."   *~Jeff Foxworthy, Comedian*

The comedian Jeff Foxworthy is famous for his one-liners about rednecks, namely, "You might be a redneck if..." Then he describes situations or symptoms that clearly pinpoint whether or not you might be a redneck. For instance, you might be a redneck if...you think the last words of the Star Spangled Banner are, "Ladies and Gentlemen, start your engines."

There is a similar question you can ask yourself in order to determine if you might be experiencing some of the symptoms of the post-retirement syndrome. Even if you feel you are not experiencing any part of a retirement depression, this section should be valuable to ponder because knowing about the issues may help to avoid them in the future.

Below are a series of post-retirement symptoms. I intentionally made the examples humorous to allow you to see how others might be viewing some of the unusual things you are doing in the early stages of retirement.

"You might be experiencing the post-retirement syndrome if..."

- You have qualified as a platinum level Internet explorer and eagerly await your next 10 hr. session in front of your wide screen monitor
- You have worn out your brand new recliner given by your spouse as a retirement gift
- You bought a chenille pillow with the inscription, "Couch Potatoes Unite"
- Your spouse has asked you to go back to work, at least three times a day for the past year
- Every day you have thought about playing golf, going fishing, visiting the mall, playing cards, working on your car, moving the furniture in the living room, clipping and filing coupons, organizing the family scrapbook...but you never got around to doing any of them, just too busy
- You have befriended your mailman, garbage man, dry cleaner delivery man, UPS driver, meter reader and anyone else who happens to come into the neighborhood
- You have conducted time and motion studies on your spouse's house cleaning routines
- You have wandered around the house looking for something to do, anything
- You have answered the phone on the first ring and talked for 30 minutes to a wrong number caller
- You regularly talk to yourself, answer your questions and respond to the answers

- You think the dog, cat or goldfish are conspiring against you and you have proof
- Your neighbors duck indoors when they see you coming
- You volunteer the time, temperature and weather because you memorize them daily
- You break things intentionally so you can fix them
- You find yourself reading content labels on cans and boxes for enjoyment
- Your children and grandchildren are afraid to ask you what's new
- You have qualified for the Senior Olympics in the advanced napping competition
- You have created a catalog to highlight your favorite senior moments
- You regularly drive by your former place of employment just to make sure it is still there
- You have watched the reruns of M.A.S.H and Jerry Seinfeld so many times you mouth the lines before they are said
- You think that daily showers are for the working class
- You can hardly wait to read the obituaries to see if you know anyone who has passed to the great beyond
- You reinstated your phone number on the national do-not-call list and anxiously await the calls from telemarketers
- You have been accused of being paranoid, but you have proof that "they" really are out to get you

If any of these symptoms sound familiar to you or your loved ones, it is highly likely that you are experiencing the post-retirement syndrome. But make sure you don't rush out and tell all your friends and neighbors, they already know.

What Triggers Post-Retirement Syndrome?

There are at least four triggers that may lead to post-retirement syndrome.

- The emotional reality that the *perception of retirement does not match the actual experiences* in the early stages of retirement.

- The sudden **change in identity**.

- The loss of a **sense of accomplishment and self-worth.**

- The *massive amount of change* that is associated with breaking habit patterns in your job or career that took years to develop.

Perception of Retirement Different than the Actual Experience

After a few weeks or months in retirement, some retirees may ask the question, *"Is that all there is to retirement?"* Many retirees enter retirement with high hopes and great expectations. They sit back and wait for retirement to come to them. Sometimes their expectation of retirement does not match the realities of their early experiences. They thought retirement would be fun and exciting; instead they feel like retirement is boring and frustrating. They thought that doing nothing would be a highly desirable, wonderful reward. Over a period of several months, sometime years, they basically do nothing. They have no plans. They just wile away their time with self-imposed habit patterns like having breakfast, reading the newspaper, watching the morning news, eating lunch, watching the soap operas, surfing the internet, watching sitcom reruns, having dinner, watching the evening news, watching a ball game or evening sitcom, going to bed, waking up the next day and repeating the same routine.

There are many unhappy retirees, especially the breadwinners who retired to a couch-potato life and have caused nothing but grief for their spouses and families as they waste away the rest of their lives.

The classic song by Peggy Lee describes the condition pretty well with the lyrics, "Is that all there is?" Peggy lamented over a series of events in her life and after each major event she intoned, "Is that all there is…to love, life, and living?" A disgruntled retiree would add, "Is that all there is to retirement?"

The answer is categorically, no. There is much more to retirement than waiting around for something to happen. There is a link between the degree of pre-retirement planning you do and the degree to which you adjust to retirement realities. Those of you who simply let retirement happen are far more likely to feel anxiety and apprehension about retirement because you failed to plan for what you really wanted to do in retirement.

If you are bored or have some misconceptions about retirement, you need to figure out what is causing these feelings. It is unlikely that you will feel any better by continuing to wait for something good to happen. You have the power to make a change in your life.

Patience is a Virtue (Sometimes)

I am reminded of a poster I saw in a sales office some years ago. There were two vultures sitting high on a tree waiting for a predator to kill something so they could swoop down and enjoy a meal. After waiting patiently for several hours, one vulture turns to the other and says…

"Patience, my butt, I'm gonna go kill me something!"

Retirement planning is very similar. There are times when you simply have to take the initiative to make it happen. No one else will do it for you. There is nothing to gain from waiting; follow the advice of the vulture and get started.

Change in Identity

Just about all retirees quickly learn that there is a major difference between your personal identities before and after you retire. There is a tendency for all of us to hang onto our pre-retirement identity. It's easier to explain who you are by describing what you formerly did. If you tell someone you were a nurse or a teacher or a pilot, they quickly classify your credentials and you feel better by the association of your former identity. If you say you are "retired", the next question is usually, "What did you do before you retired?"

People are prone to classify you on who you were, not who you are now. You may see yourself as a successful, experienced, stable, secure and wise retired senior. The rest of the world probably sees you as simply another aging retiree.

We have a tendency to transfer our previous rank and career accomplishments into our perception about the kind of person that we think we are. For instance, when a military officer retires, it is common to continue to call him or her by their highest rank, such as, "Colonel Jones" or "Sarge". There is a subtle thing in our psyche that wants to hang on to our former identity. Unfortunately the real world views us much differently.

One of my friends describes it this way, *"You are no longer who you were, you are who you are now."* You might have been a very successful person in your career but in retirement you are just you. You have no rank, no privilege, no title, and no perks, just you the person with a memory of who you once were. A great career and credentials don't get you any privileges in retirement.

Most of us begin to sense in the early months or years of retirement that few people have much interest in our former skills, capabilities, insights, opinions and accumulated years of experience and wisdom. Although it takes decades to qualify for retirement, it only takes a few weeks or months to learn that not many people really care about the collective experience and wisdom that is resident in the minds and bodies of the entire senior population.

Ironically, a person never retires from their experience and wisdom. You will take it to your grave but most of the world around you will view your credentials in retirement different than how they were viewed during your career. A retired neurosurgeon is simply that, retired.

It would seem logical that just about everyone would want to use the collective wisdom of our seniors. But the current culture is fixated with youth and the prevailing attitude is that the old-timers can't add much to the nouveau technological mindset. That is really too bad because most of the best ideas and inventions of the past century have come from the minds and wisdom of today's senior citizens.

If you feel a little neglected or think that you could be contributing more to the world, you are probably right. The challenge is to find a way that you can make a meaningful contribution that will satisfy your own needs for recognition and gratification while at the same time convincing the rest of the world that age is not a negative condition.

In the meantime, if you feel under-appreciated and under-utilized, or downright frustrated, you have probably interpreted the signs correctly and you are most likely experiencing a bit of the post-retirement syndrome.

Sense of Accomplishment and Self-Worth

One of the issues that many retirees don't realize is the role that their job and career played in developing a personal sense of accomplishment and self-worth. When the job or career suddenly ends and is not replaced with activities that compensate for this need, it is likely to trigger depression or a sense of under appreciation.

Many retirees start their retirement by throwing themselves into all kinds of fun-filled activities. For me it was golf. For you it might be tennis or shopping or fishing or playing cards or travel or dining or a host of other activities or hobbies. But at the end of the day, many retirees feel like something is missing. The missing link is that the fun-filled activities may not have adequately compensated for the sense of accomplishment and self-worth that you received from your job and career.

The big question then is, "Now what?" First, you have to realize that you are not alone and many retirees experience the same condition. Next, you need to adjust your internal gauges in terms of what should make you feel that you have accomplished something. For instance, if you are a golfer, you need to set goals for yourself that you can use to monitor your progress while celebrating each new level of accomplishment.

Most seniors need to have an "attitude adjustment" session about the role of "fun" in your life. In a nutshell, it is okay to do things purely for the fun of it. If you feel guilty about spending too much time having fun, then you were probably a victim of an inbred Judeo-Christian ethic that suggests anything that is done purely for fun must be suspect. You probably had parents who browbeat you with the need to do something useful rather than just wasting your time. Parents in our era had a very strong work ethic and expected us to have a similar ethic. There was little room for doing things purely for fun.

If the fun things continue to make you happy, don't change a thing, just continue to do what makes you happy and contented.

Eventually some retirees begin to question what really makes them feel contented and fulfilled. If you still feel the inner need for a higher level of accomplishment and personal fulfillment, then it is probably safe to suggest that you need to develop some new objectives for your retirement experience. You need to find things to do, in addition to the fun-filled activities that cause you to feel a better sense of well-being. The key to a higher level of self-worth is usually found in doing things that are more challenging. You might need to go back to work, part-time or full-time or take some classes at a local college or get involved in volunteer work or start a new business or learn a whole new trade or occupation.

For some retirees, the ultimate sense of fulfillment is achieved by engaging in activities that help others. When you begin to focus some of your time on doing things for other people, there is a new opportunity to develop a better feeling about the true purpose of life and retirement.

A golfing buddy of mine is a retired pediatrician. He spent his career caring for children, a truly fulfilling experience. But in retirement he missed the sense of accomplishment he got from the experiences with his "kids" as he calls them. At the urging of his spouse, he got involved in a religious education program at his church and found himself in the middle of young children again. He loved the experience and the children loved him. One day a pre-teen whispered to him, "You know what, Doc? You're pretty cool for an old guy!" Just think how valuable that one comment was to his personal sense of satisfaction and fulfillment.

The secret to success in retirement for many retirees is not what's in it for "me", but rather what you can do for someone else. Specifically, how can you use your time, talent and treasure to benefit others? By doing so, you are more likely to find a deep sense of satisfaction and fulfillment.

A classic example of how to achieve fulfillment is in the hearts and actions of grandmothers and grandfathers around the world. Many millions of grandparents are babysitting, caring for and nurturing their grandchildren because they want to be involved in their lives. For some, it is a form of compensation for the time they were not able to spend with their own children. For others, it is simply an act of love that is motivated purely out of a desire to be helpful and involved. Perhaps the perfect image of contentment and fulfillment is a picture of a grandparent holding a grandchild.

Massive Change in Retirement

The final trigger for post-retirement syndrome is learning how to cope with the massive amount of change that comes with retirement. Many retirees fail to anticipate how their life will change when they no longer have to get up at 6:00am and head off to work. Just think about it…what do you do when you get up? Do you shower first or read the newspaper or watch the news or turn on your computer or go for a walk? Whatever you do, it will be a change in your routine and that of your spouse or partner.

The impact of the change is particularly felt by the spouse or partner who suddenly has to adapt to a new lifestyle that involves a 24/7 relationship with the newly retired partner who may have formerly been simply an overnight guest.

In partner or married relationships, every aspect of your life will change. You and your partner will be scrutinized and evaluated on just about everything you formerly did routinely without question or concern. Suddenly someone is questioning why you keep the corn flakes on the top shelf instead of the middle shelf in the pantry.

You need to anticipate and plan for change. The newly retired partner needs to be particularly sensitive to the other partner's time and well-established habit patterns. It is always a good idea to consider yourself a guest in "their" home until you earn your full-time living privileges. It's also appropriate to ask permission before you turn the TV channel to your favorite sports program.

There are many other personal and practical changes that you will experience in the early days and months of retirement that can be resolved by prior discussion and compromise.

Perhaps the biggest change you will experience is the loss of your position, rank, privilege, title, and inner feelings of importance that your job or career provided. It may have taken years or decades to arrive at your particular position and it is not easy to be suddenly stripped of your personal trappings.

You will find it difficult to walk away from the emotional supports of your job and career. The day you retire is the day you leave all of that behind. You are no longer the person you once were, you are now a retired person and nobody now knows or probably cares about who you once were. For example, more than one politician has felt the sudden and dramatic loss of self-esteem the morning after an unsuccessful election campaign, including former Presidents of the United States who were cared for and coddled aboard Air Force One and the next day they're in the back of the plane with the rest of us.

Summary

The post-retirement syndrome affects not only the retiree but also the spouses, partners and families of unhappy retirees. When a retiree suffers through a difficult adjustment period in retirement they impact the emotional and psychological health of the entire family.

The key to breaking the malaise of the post-retirement syndrome is to replace the non-productive habit patterns with meaningful and productive activities. The place you want to start is to understand the causes of the post-retirement syndrome that triggered your behavior. It's not that you intentionally wanted to become an unproductive retiree; it's just that you failed to develop a better understanding about retirement and the role you had to play in developing a retirement plan. While you were waiting for help, you simply slipped unintentionally into the melancholy of the post-retirement syndrome.

The reality is that no one can force happiness, whether it is with money or power or prestige. Happiness starts within and emanates outwards from a satisfied and contented inner soul.

In addition, there is the potential for one's self-esteem to take a negative hit. If a person was routinely treated with respect and admiration, or if their rank in their profession warranted special attention, the sudden loss of their former perks and privileges can cause a person to lose a good deal of their self-esteem.

Key Point: Perhaps the biggest and most obvious revelation about retirement is that you get out of retirement what you plan to get out of it. Yet, ironically, many retirees are reluctant to put a pencil to pad to create a plan for what they want to do with the rest of their lives. It sounds obvious but if you don't have a reasonably comprehensive retirement plan, you have the potential to drift aimlessly through your remaining years, sort of like waiting for something good to happen. It's all up to you.

Section Two

Personalized Retirement Plan (PRP)

"It's better to look ahead and prepare than to look back and regret."
~Jackie Joiner Kersee, Athlete

Chapter 6

A New Retirement Planning Model

"Good fortune is what happens when opportunity meets with planning."
                                        ~Thomas Alva Edison

In prior generations, there was a misconception about retirement planning. People tended to get along without a formal retirement plan or they prepared a financial plan and thought that was all they needed. Many people felt that a "financial plan" and a "retirement plan" were one in the same. The difference between the two terms is much more than semantics.

A "financial plan" is about money. It is a summary of how you will manage your financial assets to ensure that you have enough money to cover all expenses in retirement. Ideally, the financial plan was initiated in the early stages of a person's career and the assets grew and compounded to the point where there is enough personal funds, and pension income, and Social Security income to allow a person to live comfortably.

A "retirement plan" deals with everything else that a person wants or needs to do to maximize their retirement experience. A retirement plan deals with what a person does with their time, talent and treasure. The financial plan is one component of a retirement plan. The financial plan helps to ensure that the senior is able to afford all the things that they planned for in their retirement plan.

One of my primary motivations in writing this book was to alert seniors to the need for preparing a retirement plan. A financial plan is important and necessary but it will not help you determine what you really want to do in your retirement. You can ill afford to simply stumble into retirement and expect that it will be a marvelous experience. You need to plan in advance what you want to do so you are able to manage your time and resources more effectively and productively.

Those who wait for retirement to come to them risk the possibility of becoming bored and disenchanted with retirement. You wouldn't think about starting a long, extended trip without a travel plan. Why would you want to embark on a ten or twenty year retirement journey without a plan? The point is that you need to prepare a retirement plan. It doesn't have to be formal or complex. You simply need to review all the pertinent issues that will affect you and your partner in your retirement years and determine how you prefer to deal with them.

In a nutshell, that is what the new *Personalized Retirement Plan* is all about (PRP for short). PRP is a logical, ten step process that guides you through a personalized assessment of wants, needs, issues, and retirement options. The end product is a summary that becomes a game plan to ensure that you are truly in charge of your retirement experience.

The thing that makes the PRP different from traditional financially-focused retirement planning is the more expansive view of retirement planning. A retiree lives with the realities of retirement 24-7 while the financial issues occupy a relatively small percentage of the total day-to-day activities. It is possible that a retiree could do a terrific job of preparing a financial plan, then turn around the next day and wonder what they should do next to find happiness and fulfillment.

Retirement is like any other major life activity; you will get out of it what you put into it. You will have a much better chance of accomplishing your retirement goals if you develop a plan to accomplish them. The PRP provides an organized way to prepare a simple, but comprehensive retirement plan that covers all aspects of the retirement experience.

The Target Audience

This book is targeted at the 60 million seniors who are already retired and the 78 million Baby Boomers who are just now beginning to enter their retirement years. The new generation of retirees will be dramatically different than prior generations. The new generation will forge a new retirement paradigm; a model that will result in a more personalized set of retirement preferences and goals. While prior generations may have waited anxiously to get their gold watch and pension, the new generation is more likely to retire early or continue working, because of desire or need, or embark on a life-changing transition to satisfy a personal dream or ambition. Where prior generations may have been preoccupied with the "security" aspects of retirement, the new generation will be more apt to explore the "social" side of the retirement experience and get involved in things that they simply enjoy doing.

The time is ripe to introduce a retirement planning approach that encourages retirees to view retirement as a series of new, exciting, and fulfilling experiences that will cause retirement to become a crowning fulfillment of their total life experience. This is *not* another book about financial planning. This book is about planning for all of the things you want or need to do in retirement to be happy, productive, and responsible.

Key Point: the need to prepare a Personalized Retirement Plan (PRP) is important whether you are a traditional retiree or a new generation retiree. Retirement planning is much like planning a wedding. It is a very special event that is going to last a very long time. If you don't plan well, something will be left out. Why take the chance of failing to discuss something really important? A PRP will help you stay on course.

If you are already retired or soon will be, congratulations you made it! The first goal of retirement is to survive long enough to get there.

Once you have opened the gate to retirement, the next step is to determine if retirement represents a fantastic opportunity or an unexpected challenge.

Retirement Requirements

There are two things that every retiree must do to prepare for retirement:

- First, you must **develop a retirement plan** that considers all aspects of retirement.

- Second, you must **revisit your financial plan** to ensure that your resources are adequate to meet your retirement goals.

There are lots of qualified financial planners who are ready, willing, and able to help you develop the financial component of your retirement plan. But, who is going to help you plan all the other things that are a part of a comprehensive retirement plan?

The Things Your Financial Planner Doesn't Ask

If you used a financial planner in the past, you have probably benefitted greatly from the professional expertise. Most financial planners do an excellent job of organizing and implementing a personalized financial plan. However, there is usually a gap between the financial plan and all the other things that a retiree needs to be aware of before embarking on their retirement journey.

There are many questions that your financial planner doesn't ask because it does not fit within the scope of their role and responsibility. Therefore, it is vital that you consider all aspects of your retirement and ask yourself the following questions:

- Where do you go to get advice and counsel on how to cope with the feelings you may have about the sudden separation from your job and career?
- How do you replace the sense of well-being and self-worth that your career provided?
- How do you create a sense of accomplishment and fulfillment without your job?
- What do you and your spouse or partner really want to do in retirement?
- How do you develop a different kind of relationship with your partner now that you are suddenly together again?
- What do you really want to do that you have not had time to do previously?
- What does your partner think about your retirement? What do they want to do? What do they want you to do?
- Are there other things you need to organize besides your finances and legal issues before you leave for the great beyond?
- How do your parents, children and grandchildren fit into your retirement plans?
- What about travel, entertainment, leisure activities, and your social life?
- What do you intend to do to take care of yourself physically and mentally?
- Are you happy with where you live? Where do you want to live? Part time or year round? Is your partner on the same page?
- What are the activities you want to get involved in? Work? Family? Community? Church? Organizations and clubs?
- Do you have any hidden dreams or fantasies that you want to consider?
- What are your strengths? Weaknesses? Opportunities? Threats?
- What is your core competency?

- How might you use your experience and wisdom to generate additional income or help others who are less fortunate?
- Do you have a desire to do something totally different than you've done so far in your career or life?
- Do you have any obligations or commitments that you must fulfill?
- What is going to make you truly happy? Your spouse or partner? Your family?
- What is your number one goal in retirement?
- Lastly, what will provide you with a sense of personal fulfillment for a life well spent?

Retirement Renaissance will provide you with the tools you can use to consider these and lots of other questions about what you want and need to do in retirement to find true happiness and personal fulfillment.

The Purpose of the Personalized Retirement Plan

The purpose of a comprehensive Personalized Retirement Plan (PRP) is to help you determine how you want to spend your **time**, how you intend to use your **talent**, and how you want to spend or use your **treasure** for maximum benefit to you and your family.

Key Point: The root cause of most adjustment problems in retirement is the lack of adequate planning. Some retirees simply allow retirement to happen with little effort on their part to guide the process. Apparently some retirees think their planning days are over when they leave their career and go into retirement. Retirement planning is vital to a successful retirement.

The lack of retirement planning is rather odd because no one would build a house without a blueprint. No one would start a business without a business plan. No one should retire without a financial plan.

Yet there are millions of retirees who are wandering into the wonderful world of retirement without a clue about what they really want to do to achieve true happiness and fulfillment.

If you don't create a Personalized Retirement Plan, you put at risk the most potentially rewarding and fulfilling part of your life. Some of the reluctance or determination to create a retirement plan is predetermined by the kind of person you are or have been. It is unlikely that you will change your personality in retirement. Therefore, there are several different types of people who end up at the gate to retirement.

Types of Retirees

Read through the descriptions and determine which category you belong to. It will help you develop a better understanding about your present condition and develop a better perspective about the need for retirement planning.

The Prepared—if you are completely happy in retirement or if you're not yet retired but you have already mapped out a Personalized Retirement Plan, including a detailed financial plan, then you probably don't need this book, unless you might want to critique your planning process to make sure you didn't leave anything out. If you're satisfied, just relax and enjoy your retirement. Although this might represent the ideal situation, there are very few retirees who are totally prepared for retirement.

The Unprepared—this book will have particular value for all seniors who have not yet prepared a comprehensive PRP or have been looking for something to help in the planning process. Many of you may be reluctant to develop a retirement plan either because you may be having second thoughts about retirement, or the traditional view of retirement, or you haven't as yet taken the time to sit down and think about retirement. If you have been putting off the inevitable, this book can be of enormous help in organizing your thinking and putting some needed structure in your planning process.

Retirement planning is one of the most important tasks you can do before you start your retirement. Yet not everyone does it. Many people simply wait to see what happens. But, you wouldn't think about buying a new home without a detailed discussion and plan. You wouldn't think about moving to another state without much thought and comparisons. You wouldn't cash in your investments without a whole lot of advice and counsel. Then why are some retirees reluctant to talk through what they would like to do in retirement?

The Concerned—if you have some concerns or trepidations about retirement, take comfort in the fact that there are many other fellow retirees in your same shoes who are standing on the doorstep to retirement and may not want to retire or might prefer to ease into retirement gradually or maybe not at all.

If you are having second thoughts about when or whether you should retire, you are like many others who have come to the realization that you might need to continue working to maintain your standard of living or you simply love your job and don't want to stop working. You may realize that you have spent several decades developing your job skills and you want to continue working because you are finally at the top of your game. You and your spouse and family may have sacrificed a great deal to get you to this position. It would not be normal if you did not have at least some second thoughts about retirement.

The Undecided—another common concern involves those of you who are undecided about what you really want to do in retirement. You may feel that the typical retirement thing is just not enough to keep you motivated and satisfied. You need to investigate your options and develop a more satisfying and compelling plan for retirement.

It is okay to be undecided. The PRP will help you get your thoughts together so you can develop a plan that is more in line with your feelings and attitudes about retirement.

The Unbridled Enthusiasts—there are also a great many future retirees who are literally counting down the days to their retirement party. If you are one of these happy and contented souls, make sure you look beyond the first few months or years of retirement. All those things you are planning to do might not be enough to satisfy your needs over an extended period of time. Once the thrill of the new camper or motor home or boat fades away, you may wake up one day and realize there is much more to life than hunting or fishing or shopping or traveling.

For instance, a dentist friend retired, sold the home, bought a giant motor home and took off to explore the United States. About a year or so later, they were tired of driving and settled down in a desert retirement community in the Southwest with a golf course and year-round great weather.

If you identified with one or more of the above types of retirees, you can take comfort in the fact that there are a great many retirees just like you. The bottom line is that each type of retiree needs to start preparing a PRP. You gain nothing by waiting. Retirement is like aging, it happens whether you like it or not.

Key Point: the more you can learn about retirement, in advance, and the more you can plan for all contingencies in retirement, the better chance you will have of experiencing a rewarding and fulfilling retirement.

Chapter 7

Personalized Retirement Plan Explained

"A good plan, executed now, is better than a perfect plan next week."
~General George S. Patton

The creation of a Personalized Retirement Plan (PRP) is a somewhat structured, but simple, process designed to help you organize your thoughts and actions about all the components in a retirement plan. In effect, it answers the question about where to start and how to organize the process. The plan consists of ten steps that encompass all aspects of retirement planning. The purpose of the Personalized Retirement Plan is to serve as a guide and outline to help you organize and simplify the process of preparing a retirement plan.

This chapter will explain the need to develop a Personalized Retirement Plan and provide an explanation about the ten steps in the PRP.

Need For a Personalized Retirement Plan

When a senior nears the traditional retirement age, there is a wealth of information and resources available to help deal with the financial side of retirement planning. Many companies offer internal assistance and there are a great many financial planners who can help a retiree determine if their nest egg will be sufficient to carry them through the anticipated years of their retirement. Even those with minimum resources can find valuable aids to assist in the process since much has been written and made available on the subject.

Apparently there is an assumption that if the financial side of retirement planning is in order then everything else will somehow fall into place. But the financial planning is only one important component of retirement planning. The practical side of retirement is equally or perhaps more important. You need to determine what you want to do with your time, talent and resources in retirement. Then you have to prepare yourself and your partner for the psychological impact of retiring. Take it from an experienced retiree that you will be involved in a lot more than just taking care of your financial resources.

If you don't develop a retirement game plan, then retirement will be nothing more than a calculated risk or gamble. You may stumble into happiness or you might end up in a state of disillusionment and withdrawal. If you want to maximize the potential that retirement represents, you must create a plan to guide you through the various challenges and opportunities.

Another saying comes to mind: the longest journey starts with the first step. You are encouraged to take the first step to create a retirement plan that captures your ambitions and dreams. Don't waste a lot of time procrastinating about starting or evaluating all the various alternatives because you will find that "time flies" in your retirement years. More than one retiree has said, "If I had known I was going to be this busy in retirement, I would have started sooner!"

Mutual Planning Process

Retirement planning must be a mutual process between spouses or partners. The initial prerequisite of the PRP is to help spouses or partners establish a stronger and more compatible communication process that will serve as the platform for discussing and evaluating a whole series of options and alternatives, much like you went through in creating your financial plan. Many couples find that the process of sitting down and talking openly about their wants and needs in retirement was one of the most important benefits of the PRP process because it brought them closer together and more able to develop a mutually beneficial plan. For some, the process has become a renewal or renaissance experience.

The fact is that if you can't talk to your spouse or partner about your desires, dreams and feelings at this point in your relationship, there is little hope for you to truly enjoy a rewarding, fulfilling and mutually compatible retirement. It is highly probable that your retirement will be a one-sided affair with one partner doing what they want and the other simply tagging along for the ride.

Only after you establish effective communication can the planning partners address their feelings about wants and needs during their retirement years. You will see once you get into the plan that the issues are highly personal and will require some real effort by both partners to get to the point where each partner can express what is really in his or her heart.

For instance, the PRP will ask that the partners talk about their death. I assure you that no one is excited about this subject, but it has to be discussed and can only be discussed when the partners are able to really communicate effectively.

Regardless of the level of communication in a marriage or partnership prior to retirement, this plan is designed to bring out the really important things that you need to discuss when planning your retirement. It suggests that the partners engage in a somewhat structured dialog that is designed to get all of the issues out on the table for discussion.

One difference you might observe in this plan is that the financial planning component comes last. This is intentional because I believe that the partners have to first determine what they want and need to do before they determine how much it might cost them. The sequencing of this last step is designed to ensure that your appetite for activity agrees with your resources.

Personalized Retirement Plan (PRP) Steps

Personalized Retirement Plan (PRP) consists of ten steps or stages. Each step is a building block that identifies key issues that need to be discussed and resolved. The answers are written into the PRP workbook. When all ten steps are discussed and agreed to, the workbook becomes the official Retirement Plan.

The ten steps are organized into four categories: personal, psychological, physiological, and practical. Each of the planning steps is described in more detail in subsequent chapters.

Personal Planning Steps

❑ **Step 1—Wants and Needs**—identify and distinguish between what you *want* to do and what you *need* to do in retirement. This step deals with the difference between wants and needs, the words are not interchangeable. Wants deal with desires and dreams. Needs deal with things that must be done and won't go away in retirement. You might want to tour Europe but you need to care for an aging parent, there is a difference. The intent is to array a series of things you want to do and things that you need to do. Once you understand the requirements, then you can begin to develop a plan to prioritize the activities. The discussion provides examples of the typical issues facing retirees and provides the opportunity to determine your true inner feelings about things that are important and necessary for you to accomplish in retirement.

❑ **Step 2—Obligations and Commitments**—this step deals with obligations and commitments that influence your retirement planning. All retirees arrive at the gate to retirement with a great deal of personal baggage that you and your partner have accumulated during your careers and family life. This section helps you to identify and prioritize the various commitments that must become a part of your retirement plan. For instance, you can't walk away from a special needs child or sometimes a family business or people who depend on your for financial or moral support. This step also addresses other key commitments that deal with family, church, and community, civic, social, and personal issues.

❑ **Step 3—Personal Inventory**—this step helps you to verify your strengths, weaknesses, opportunities and threats. As you are contemplating your options in retirement, it helps to review your strengths to determine what you are really good at. Most people are good at a lot of things but usually there are one or two areas in which you excel; these areas represent a person's core competencies. One of the ways to achieve a deep sense of satisfaction and fulfillment is to use your strengths and core competencies in retirement to do things that you've always wanted to do but never had quite enough time. For instance, if you were a star salesperson, your core competency is probably in the area of strong human relations skills. Once you identify your true strengths, you can then determine how you can use your strength to achieve a greater sense of satisfaction and fulfillment, or possibly to supplement your income or simply for enjoyment. It is a common practice for a business or new venture to develop a "SWOT" analysis; namely, the discussion and identification of an organization's strengths, weaknesses, opportunities, and threats. The same principles can be applied to help you determine your personal strengths and weaknesses, opportunities or threats to your overall wellbeing. The intent is to help you determine what you might want to consider doing in retirement for either enjoyment or for financial gain. You will develop a better understanding about your strengths and weaknesses so that you can evaluate your retirement options and focus on those things that you do really well, including the things that represent your core competencies.

In addition, you need to assess any opportunities that are staring you in the face that you have always wanted to pursue. Lastly, you need to identify any threats that you need to avoid or plan around.

Psychological Planning Steps

❑ **Step 4—Life after Retirement**—you need to learn how to adjust to life after retirement and recognize that a great many new retirees experience anywhere from a mild to a severe depression in the early phases of retirement. It makes sense to anticipate and plan for how to cope with the sudden change from the workaday world to the retirement world. There is nothing wrong with experiencing sadness about leaving your job and colleagues. The important thing is to make sure that the melancholy doesn't persist and create serious problems for you and everyone around you. The key is to find substitutes for the rewards and self-gratification you received from your job and career. The substitutes may not be exactly the same but it is important to feel good about who you are and what you are doing. There can be great joy and satisfaction in getting a task completed that has been on the "to do" list for months or years. So what if it's only cleaning out the basement and not inventing a new miracle drug, if it makes you feel a sense of accomplishment, it will help you to cope with the adjustments to retirement.

❑ **Step 5—Goals in Life**—this step challenges you to validate or revalidate your goals in life. Long before you ever thought about retirement, you were subconsciously thinking about what you wanted to accomplish in life; whether it was in your career, within your family, or financially, or spiritually. You thought about what you wanted to do or who you wanted to become. As you enter retirement, it is appropriate that you look back on your original goals and ambitions and evaluate your progress. If you are truly satisfied with what you've accomplished, then you might want to consider creating some additional goals for the balance of your life. If you have fallen short of your goals, you might want to use your retirement years to fulfill your original ambitions. At the end of the day, the goal for everyone is to feel a sense of satisfaction and fulfillment about one's life. Many retirees strive to achieve a higher level of fulfillment by using their time, talent, and treasure to enrich other people's lives. This section helps you understand the broader concept of fulfillment and provides examples of how you can plan to achieve a truer sense of personal fulfillment.

Physiological Planning Steps

❑ **Step 6—Physical Conditioning**—this step addresses the need to maintain or improve your physical condition. By the time most people reach their 50s or 60s there is an increased potential for various health challenges. This suggests the need to make a realistic and honest assessment of your physical condition and incorporate the facts and requirements into your plan. For instance, if one partner has high blood pressure or diabetes, the condition suggests the need for specific regimens or programs to help alleviate the condition so that it does not become a preventable issue later in retirement. You only have one body, an aging body at that, and you need to devote more of your time in retirement to keeping it healthy to offset the impact of aging.

❑ **Step 7—Mental Conditioning**—this step focuses on the need to continually exercise and utilize your brain resources to achieve a high level of mental conditioning. The power of a person's brain comes from the collective experiences of lifelong learning. The experience and wisdom that a person brings to retirement is probably the most important asset, greater by far than any financial reserves. This step suggests that you need to exercise your brain as you simultaneously exercise your body. A healthy mind and body go hand in hand to allow you to enjoy additional years of active retirement. Nobody wants to be sick or a burden on your spouse or family. The secret is to stay healthy, mentally and physically. Many of the memory issues and "senior moments" can be lessened by doing routines that exercise the brain and improve mental acuity. The old saying, "use it or lose it" is true. This steps lists some of the many things you can do to maintain a good mental condition.

Practical Planning Steps

❑ **Step 8—Lifestyle, Location and Leisure**—this is a highly practical step to help you determine your personal preferences for lifestyle, location and leisure. One of the really important discussions you need to have with your planning partner is to determine how you want to live (your lifestyle), where you want to live, and how you want to spend your time. There are lots of reasons why people are thrust into a lifestyle that may not be their preferred lifestyle. When a person is transferred to a major city and becomes an urban dweller or commuter, they assume an urban lifestyle that may be exactly opposite of the down home, small town mentality that they prefer. Retirement provides the opportunity to assess your lifestyle and determine exactly how you want to live your life and where you want to live.

The fact is that many retirees from harsher climates can hardly wait to retire and relocate to the Sunbelt. Other retirees build their retirement goals around an activity; for instance, moving to a senior friendly community with golf courses, tennis, and lots of social activities. This section helps you to identify and talk through the pros and cons of relocation and the other issues involved in a preoccupation with one or more activities. The intent is to help you decide what is in the best interest of both parties and the extended families.

❑ **Step 9—Exit Strategy**—this step deals with the difficult topic of death and dying. You can't avoid reality. You will die, hopefully not anytime soon, so you must develop your "Exit Strategy"; or, what you want to happen after you die. If you retire at age 60 and the average life expectancy is 80, you are officially in the last quarter of your life. The key point is not to dwell on the reality, rather take the time to acknowledge and plan for it, then to do everything possible to maximize your retirement experience. This step leads you through all the things you need to consider before you die in order to make the transition much easier on your spouse and family; including all the ticklish legal, medical, family, and personal issues. The creation of your exit strategy is one of the most important components of your retirement plan. You have an obligation to discuss and communicate the details of your exit strategy with your planning partner, the family and your professional advisors.

☐ **Step 10—Financial Plan Integration**—the last step deals with integrating your financial plan into your overall retirement plan. Hopefully you developed a financial plan early in your career to provide you and your partner with adequate resources in retirement. If you did, then the task is to incorporate that plan into your retirement plan. If you didn't, then you need to stop what you are doing and seek a financial advisor who can help you determine what you need to do to protect your future security. I intentionally placed financial integration as the last step, not to lessen its importance, rather to highlight the need to focus on the other nine steps so that you will have a better understanding about your financial requirements. For instance, if you determine that you want or need to do certain things and you don't have the financial resources, then it becomes important that you identify how you will fund your aspirations. You should not eliminate things you want or need to do simply because you don't now have the resources. You simply need to determine how you might go about getting the additional resources so that you can fulfill the goals of your PRP.

Key Point: I don't imply by putting financial planning in the last position that you should wait until you retire to start your financial planning. You need to start the financial planning process early in your career so you can provide the resources you need during your career, marriage, and retirement. This last step is more of a review than the creation of a financial plan. The purpose is to help you determine if your financial resources are in line with the requirements of your retirement plan.

A Word about Planning

For those of you who would like to create some distance between you and anything that smacks of planning, especially those familiar with the rigors of corporate or organizational planning, don't worry because you can predetermine the extent of your planning. Don't allow the idea of a somewhat formal structure to deter you from creating your PRP. A simple plan is far better than no plan at all.

The process of working with your spouse or partner to create your PRP is almost as important as the plan itself. If you follow the steps of the PRP, it will cause you to discuss the core issues that will lead to happiness and fulfillment in retirement.

On the other hand, there is no need to develop an overly detailed PRP. Retirement planning should not be overly structured so that the plan overpowers the intent. The idea is to enjoy life but to organize it in such a way that you actually realize your hopes, dreams, and aspirations. At the end of the day, you will be happy if you can say, like Frank Sinatra did, "I did it my way!" The only way you can do it your way is to have a game plan, your personal PRP.

Chapter 8

Personalized Retirement Plan:
Step #1—Wants and Needs

"There are only two tragedies in life: one is not getting what one wants, and the other is getting it. "   *~Oscar Wilde*

A third grade boy raises his hand in the classroom and asks, "Teacher, can I go to the restroom?" The teacher replies, "Yes, you probably *can* but you *may* not." The young boy looks quizzically at the teacher and in that instance is introduced to the semantics of the English language.

There is a significant difference between "can" and "may." Yes, you can, but no, you may not. The word "can" deals with ability to do something while the word "may" deals with the determination of whether you can do something or the authority to do it. Yet we tend to use the terms interchangeably. The same is true for the words "want" and "need". It is very important that you understand the difference because what you *want* in retirement could be much different than what you *need* in retirement.

Wants vs. Needs

What do you **want** to do to have fun, enjoy life, and achieve personal fulfillment in retirement? The emphasis is on the word "want" as opposed to what you "need" to do. The difference is real, not semantic.

The dictionary defines "**want**" as the state of lacking something that is *desired*. The synonyms for "want" would include: wish for, desire, crave, covet or yearn for. The word want implies the desire to have something that you don't now have or to do something that you have not yet done but always wanted to do. The key word is "desire".

The dictionary definition of "**need**" is the lacking of something *necessary*. A need implies something that is absolutely necessary for survival like food, water, shelter, or financial resources. The word "want" implies something that you would *like* to have or do. Want is "like to have" and need is "must have." The key word is "necessary".

When put into the context of retirement planning, the purpose of determining your "**wants**" is to dig deep into your inner self and bring to the surface all of the things that you have always wanted to do, or have, or be involved in. The reality is that you have a finite number of years to turn your dreams into reality.

What Do You Want?

Remember when you were a little boy or girl and you were asked the time-honored question, "What do you *want* to be when you grow up?" Way back then most of us didn't have a clue as to what we really wanted. Some of us may have expressed our career goals as a part of our childhood fantasies, like playing in the major leagues or becoming a Hollywood star or President of the United States.

Whatever it was, most of us were merely taking stabs in the dark. While a few may have actually achieved their fantasy dreams, some of the responses were influenced by the careers of parents or the family environment. For instance, if your father or mother was a doctor or farmer or teacher, you may have instinctively said that you wanted to be like them. It is highly likely that in some cases the aspirations became a self-fulfilling prophecy as a result of the reinforcement from the family environment. A similar thing can be said about all of the children who followed in their parents footsteps in a family owned business.

On the other hand, many people made decisions about their career and life wants based on external influences rather than deep inner motivations. I suspect there are lots of retirees who never made conscious decisions about what they really wanted to do or become in their careers, they just sort of left things up to fate or external forces. For instance, there were many men who became career soldiers after they got a taste of the military as a result of the draft. Or, in the post-World War II era, many young people went to work at any good paying job and ended up spending a career without ever determining if that was what they really wanted to do. There were lots of career dreams that were put on the back burner involuntarily.

Another major career diversion occurred to the many of millions of women who sacrificed their professional careers to become full-time mothers and housewives. Although their home life may have been extremely rewarding, there are many of them who still carry with them the dreams of an unfulfilled career opportunity.

The point is that some people end up at the door of retirement with deep, inner feelings about what they were not able to do or accomplish in their lives. The unquenched desire is there whether it was a major career issue or simpler wants about activities or things. Therefore, it is absolutely vital that you express your inner feelings about what you want to do or have during your retirement years.

Keep in mind that retirement represents the culmination of your life and now is not the time to hold back on anything that you really want. However, some of your wants may not be practical or affordable, none the less it is important that you express your inner feelings so that you can evaluate whether or not you still want to or are capable of doing them.

For instance, I had a boyhood fantasy of becoming a professional field goal kicker in the National Football League. When I was a kid, my idol was Lou "The Toe" Groza. I watched every Cleveland Browns football game for years and years. Every day I practiced kicking field goals in a large municipal park down the street. I imagined each kick sailing through the goal posts as time expired. Unfortunately I dislocated my right hip and was not able to fulfill my fantasy. But, the inner feeling remained with me. Eventually I had to get it out on the table and admit that I was no longer going to fulfill one of my most important childhood dreams.

On the other hand, there is nothing wrong with stating your dream because it may lead to some other activity that might satisfy the intent of the want. For example, there are lots of retirees in Florida who flock to the spring training ballparks to get their fix while they fulfill their boyhood dreams about becoming a major league baseball player. There are also many instances where a senior expressed a want that they ended up doing, in spite of the warnings about their age and potential dangers. For example, some of the brave paratroopers on D-Day wanted to make one last memorial parachute jump into the fields of Normandy on the 50th anniversary of the invasion of Europe. Although the "authorities" tried their best to talk them out of it, the survivors, in their 70s and 80s, went through with their jump and fulfilled their dreams.

Key Point: You have to understand the difference between what you WANT to do and what you NEED to do in retirement.

Key Wants and Needs

There are several key categories that will allow you to review the things that you may want or need to do as you develop the first step of your retirement plan. There are several categories of activity that will help you hone in on what you might want or need to do: work, family, social, church and community.

1. **Work Wants and Needs**—perhaps the most important issue you will discuss is whether or not you want to work or need to continue working in order to sustain your lifestyle, or to cover

your expenses, or to save for future needs, or simply because you like to work. Your financial planner will be able to quickly determine if your retirement nest egg is sufficient to carry you through your retirement years.

If your nest egg is not sufficient, then continuing to work is more of a need. If you have sufficient resources, then work might become a desirable option. In either situation, you must determine if you need to work or simply want to work.

There are also other issues that are triggered by your decision to work or not work. The fact that you have been working for several decades has created an inner attitude or feeling about work itself. For instance, one of the primary causes of the post-retirement syndrome is the inability of a retiree to adjust to not working, specifically the loss of the feeling of satisfaction, accomplishment, and self-esteem that comes from work and career. Therefore, the issue of work or the need/want to work is a compelling issue for many retirees. In a later chapter we will deal with the need to work but the focus here is on retirees who want to work or have a very strong desire to work.

Work Ethic

Many retirees in the Greatest Generation (the World War II era) and the Silent Generation era (post-World War II), including many Baby Boomers, inherited a very strong work ethic from their parents. Many kids born in the 1930 to 1950 timeframe started their working careers as newspaper carriers, supermarket bag boys, caddies, baby-sitters, grass-cutters, drugstore clerks, even pinsetters in the old bowling alleys, and many other creative occupations. These generations were brought up with the awareness that work was good and necessary because everyone had to earn his or her keep. Not many kids back then got allowances and the only way to have pocket money was to earn it.

In my own youth I was a caddie, a grocery stock boy, a drug store clerk, a soda jerk (back when there were soda fountains), a billing clerk in a building supply company, a delivery and stock boy for a sporting goods store and the usual baby-sitting and lawn care jobs. I was not an exception because my sisters and all the other kids in our neighborhood worked at part-time jobs long before any of us started our careers.

As a result, the idea of working was an assumed imperative. Eventually when people in this generation started their careers they were well prepared to throw themselves into their jobs. It was not uncommon for people to start with a company and retire from the same company. I had two uncles who started their working careers without going to high school and they both worked 50 years for the same company. There was a sense of loyalty, commitment and security in pledging your career to one company.

Psychological Impact

Although things are dramatically different today, there are lots of old-timers who retire physically but are unable to cope with the psychological impact because work has always been a pivotal part of their life. They quickly learn that retirement does not satisfy the inner craving or desire to work and provide, a motivation that is ingrained in their psyche.

My grandfather felt that work was not only something that he wanted to do; he felt it was an important necessity in his life. Therefore, he never retired. He just kept working because he liked to work.

If you identify with this condition, then you have to face the issue and decide how you will satisfy your desire to work, whether you need to financially or not. Once you make this decision, the only issue is to determine what kind of work you want to do.

One option would be to simply continue working at your present career, whether full or part-time. The amount you work would depend on the level of your desire and your financial condition. Also, you need to factor in the wants of your partner relative to the amount of time you spend working. Keep in mind that retirement is a mutual partnership. Both partners have to agree on what they will do relative to work and retirement.

Another option might be to find a new job that matches your strengths and core competencies. For instance, I met a retiree in Florida recently who retired from a large transportation company where he was a scheduling manager. He and his spouse moved to Florida and he intended to play golf the rest of his life. He soon got bored and realized that he really liked to work so he found a job as a starter at a private golf club that allowed him to capitalize on his scheduling skills while also providing him with a place to play golf on his days off. It was a great match for his wants and his core competencies.

My wife does vision screening for pre-K children to identify potential vision problems. She was not able to fulfill her career goal as a registered nurse but in retirement she is experiencing a tremendous sense of satisfaction by working at something she enjoys that is also aligned with her core competency, namely an ability to help and care for people.

Gauge Your Level of Wanting to Work

The following questions should help you gauge how much you might want to work. Discuss your answers with your partner and then determine if you feel a desire to work in some capacity as a part of your PRP.

- Do you really miss your job? The people? The environment? The activity?

- Did your job provide you with the most satisfaction and fulfillment?
- Are you able to get a sense of satisfaction and accomplishment in the things you now do in retirement? More or less than when you worked?
- Do you feel that you are under-utilizing your skills and capabilities?
- If your former boss called and offered your old job, would you take it?
- Do you find yourself experimenting with various activities that you hope will provide you with a sense of satisfaction and accomplishment that you experienced in your old job?
- Have you determined that you really like to work? Is work an important part of your life?

If these questions triggered a sense that you really do miss working, then you have to discuss what you will do to satisfy your want or desire to work. Incidentally, there is nothing wrong with making a decision to return to work, in some capacity, as a part of your PRP. Just because you are retired, does not mean that you can't or shouldn't work if you really want to.

More and more seniors are returning to the workplace because they want to work. If you still want to work, there are countless opportunities for you to find rewarding and fulfilling jobs. You might not be able to find an exact match for your skills and competencies, but you will probably feel a whole lot better by doing what you enjoy.

For instance, Publix Supermarkets in Florida hires seniors as cashiers and bag "boys" and they have brought a sense of youth and energy and enthusiasm that is absolutely contagious. One of the in-demand jobs is the "greeter" in Wal-Mart and other chains.

If you want to work, there are lots of opportunities.

Need to Work

There is a difference between your "want" to work and your "need to work". You may want to work simply because you miss your old job or you want to keep yourself busy with meaningful things to do. On the other hand, you might need to work if your retirement nest egg has taken a serious hit from the financial crisis. The difference is illustrated by this quote:

"I will try to follow the advice that a university president once gave a commencement speaker. He said to think of a speaker as the body at an Irish wake. They need you there in order to have the party, but no one expects you to say very much."
~Anthony Lake, National Security Advisor

Sometimes there is a fine line between want and need when a person wants to do something so bad that it appears to be a need or requirement. In this instance you have to determine if you need to work because of some overwhelming requirement.

Another example of the need to work is when an unexpected medical or other emergency depletes the family financial resources. There are some seniors who are returning to the workforce to earn additional money in order to maintain a certain standard of living that was threatened by economic fluctuations, inflation or higher than anticipated cost of living.

Another valid reason for working is to earn extra money to pay for a new expense that was not previously planned. For instance, a second home in a warmer winter location or a seasonal rental or a new car.

There are lots of valid reasons why you might need to work. Most of them involve your financial condition and resources. If you have developed a financial plan for your retirement and your financial advisor suggests that your nest egg may not last long enough, then you have to determine how you will earn additional money.

When You Decide to Return to Work

There are lots of options for seniors who want to return to the workforce. The key issue is to find something to work at that is compatible with your strengths and core competencies. Be sure to read the chapter on core competencies to get some ideas about what you might be capable of doing.

That doesn't mean that you have to look for a job that is commensurate with the kind of job you enjoyed during your career. There are lots of seniors who are working at hourly positions in retailing or the service trades because they enjoy the job, even though they may be overly qualified.

There was a commercial by McDonalds a few years ago that showed a retiree in a McDonald's uniform hustling around the store doing task after task. Finally he was shown cleaning the front door of the restaurant. After he put the finishing touches on it, he smiled and said, "I don't know how they ever got along without me!"

There were actually two messages in the advertisement. First, it was a recruitment message to attract seniors to work in their stores. Second, it was a subtle attempt to change the image of the typical McDonalds clerk from a scrub-faced teenager to a more mature senior citizen. McDonalds, along with other major companies, are beginning to realize that the retired senior population represents one of the biggest and best labor pools for prospective new employees.

If you are one of the millions of retirees who must work or need to return to the workforce, it is absolutely vital that you not think of the requirement as an indictment of you or your personal situation. It might turn out to be a blessing in disguise. All it means is that you will have an opportunity to continue being active in the pursuit of something that you will enjoy and benefit from.

2. **Family Wants and Needs**—there's an old Irish saying, *"An Irishman gets more Irish the further he gets from Ireland."* I never realized how much my extended family and close friends meant until we moved 500 miles from my original home and heritage.

We moved to Atlanta in 1979 and most of our extended family and friends were in Ohio. At first we were busy making new friends and meeting new neighbors so we didn't have time to look back. Eventually we all began to miss the family reunions and friendly get-togethers, especially during the Holidays. It seems like the older we get the more we feel the need to get closer to the people who were an important part of our early lives. It may also be possible that retirement represents a time when we can reflect more easily on some of the more important things in life.

This section will focus on possible wants and needs in your family. The family relationships are usually the closest and sometimes the most difficult to confront. The reality is that we choose our friends, God gives us our relatives and there is nothing we can do about it.

Family Wants

If there are relatives who are important to you then you should make a decision that you *want* to maintain or enhance the relationships. During retirement you should have time to patch up or build relationships but you must first determine that you want to do it. Keep in mind that the clock is ticking and if there is something you want to do, you should do it, don't wait because either you or your relative might not be available when you decide it is time.

If you have ever lost a relative or close friend to a sudden, tragic event, you know how you felt when you realized that you were not able to see them one more time or to make amends or to say goodbye.

Many families get scattered to the wind as result of marriage, careers, and fate. If time and distance have stepped between what was once a close and rewarding relationship, then you should make the conscious decision that you want to rebuild the relationship. I don't imply or suggest that you should get close to all of your relatives, especially if that is not your style. But I do suggest rather strongly that a close relationship with a sibling or compatible family member can be one of the most rewarding experiences in your life.

Some of the most potentially rewarding opportunities in retirement are to improve relationships within your family because you *want* to, not because you *need* to. The task of improving relationships is much more difficult because you have to go outside yourself and get involved in the attitudes and feelings of other people.

Family Needs

If the issue that created an interpersonal problem is something major, it will require a great deal of tact and diplomacy to even broach the subject with the other party. For instance, there are parents and children and siblings who have not talked to each other for years because of some issue that was perceived to be of great consequence at the time. It is highly possible that the issue may no longer be as consequential as it once was.

Think about all of the young men and women who ran away from home because their parents could not forgive such things as a teen age pregnancy or smoking pot or guzzling too much beer. How about the personal hurt that exists in many families where the children were not able to satisfy the demands or standards of their parents? How about the many people who have abandoned or avoided contact with their families for no legitimate reason? There is a plethora of reasons why families stop communicating and loving each other and many of the problems have resulted in separation or abandonment. Unfortunately, these scars can linger for years and years.

The issues that involve parents and siblings are in the category of things that *need* to be resolved. No parent or child should go to their grave with the burden of a failed relationship. Even if the cause of the separation was criminal or so egregious to prevent a normal relationship, there is still an underlying need to rationalize the event in your own mind and forgive the person even if you can never forgive the incident. Remember: to forgive is divine. It might be the most difficult thing you will ever do in your life, but you will feel better and you will be able to proceed with building a satisfying and rewarding retirement.

The blood relationships tend to be the strongest because we have an innate instinct to take care of those who are close to us and there is no one closer than a person who shares your same bloodline. They know you and you know them in a way that others will never be able to imitate or replicate.

For instance, I recently attended a family reunion and talked to some cousins who I had not seen for decades. After only a brief period of conversation we began to reminisce about things that we shared many years prior that only those inside our family had ever experienced. It was a very special, warm and rewarding feeling.

Key Point: you have only one family. Whether large or small, closely knit or out of communication, you need to do whatever you can to re-establish contact or patch up relationships while you are still able. You will feel so much better, so will they.

3. **Social Wants and Needs**—on the social side of life, there are a select number of people who you classify as your best friends. These are the people you treasure. These are the people you want to spend time with. These are the people who you will want to be with, physically and socially for the rest of your life.

As wonderful as these relationships may be, the reality is that at other points in your life you enjoyed very similar relationships with other sets of friends that have somehow been put on hold for a variety of reasons. When you were kids, you had close friends that were the most important people in your life. When you went off to elementary school, then high school, then college, then early in your career, you developed relationships that you thought would never end.

One of the bittersweet experiences in life is to attend a class reunion. Although everyone truly enjoys seeing and renewing relationships with people who once were your closest friends, you are also saddened that your life's path has caused you to distance yourself from these important relationships.

Your retirement planning provides you with an opportunity to go back over your entire life and recall all of those people who were once your best friends and determine which of them you want to re-establish relationships with. You might learn that some of your old best friends might once again become your very best friends.

The modern day technology makes it relatively easy to track down people so there is no excuse why you can't try to find a long lost friend, if you really want to.

Petty Issues

In addition to the serious types of relationship issues, there are also lots of petty issues that have created major relationship problems within families and friends. Most of the petty issues involve hurt feelings or pride. Just about every human being has at one time or another hurt someone's feelings, or themselves been deeply hurt, either intentionally or unintentionally. It is a darn shame that we are not able to avoid the problem but even more remarkable is that we can allow the condition to fester for years or decades without doing something about it.

How many people have held grudges because they were snubbed or made fun of way back in grade school or high school or college? How many stares and visual daggers have been thrown because someone was not invited to a dance or party or social event? How many tears have been shed as a result of uncaring or unintentional comments about a person's appearance? How many times has gossip destroyed a relationship or possibly ruined a career? Who amongst us has never been offended by criticism whether deserved or not? Few people go through life without offending someone or being offended by relatives or friends or career associates.

If you have interpersonal issues that need to be improved or enhanced, now is the time to do something about them. Not only should you go back and clean the board of past sins and offenses, you need to make the effort because it is the right thing to do. You should not leave this earth holding grudges or resentments that could be resolved by a phone call or handshake. Your retirement years represent an opportunity similar to a confessional in which you can wipe the slate clean by admitting your errors and asking for forgiveness.

When you decide what relationships you need to improve, the most important action point is to figure out what you will do to take the first step. Sometimes the best approach is to simply call or write someone and let him or her know that you want to take the first step. Don't wait until you determine the best possible approach, just do it. It is likely that the other person will appreciate your initiative. Remember that life is too short to harbor ill will or grudges.

4. **Spiritual Wants and Needs**—a preacher stood at the pulpit one Sunday and announced to his congregation, "I have good news and bad news. The good news is we have enough money to pay for our new building program. The bad news is that it's still out there in your pockets."

Some of my fondest memories from my childhood involved things that happened in our church and neighborhood. Back then the church and neighborhood was the center of the community for most people. One of my favorite days of the year was the annual church festival. It sure wasn't Disneyland but the sights and sounds and smells will live in my memory.

This section deals with the things you might want to do in retirement that involve spiritual and religious needs. First, I would like to give a disclaimer or personal point of view about the inclusion of spiritual or religious related things in your PRP. Most people have or once had some kind of relationship or involvement with a church or religious institution. For all of you who are active in your church or religious beliefs, this chapter may be very important in terms of rounding out the things that you might want to do in your retirement.

For those of you who have fallen away from formal church activity or who proclaim no religious beliefs, I will not attempt to convince you to return to church or soften your outlook about religion in general. All I would suggest is that you briefly examine the motivations behind your judgment to lessen the role of religion in your life and consider if the principles are still valid. After all, one of the most personal and cherished of your possessions is our right to determine your religious beliefs or lack of them.

There are lots of seniors who have fallen away from an earlier commitment to a church or religious belief because they simply got involved in other things, not because they had fundamental differences of opinion about their religion. The reality of embracing a religion is that a person has to make a time commitment to attend services and keep up to date on their beliefs. It is much easier to go through life without allocating time to your church or religious beliefs. But those people who have maintained a commitment to their church and religion continue to do so because they believe that the benefits far outweigh the time commitment and challenges of a secular world.

If you have stopped practicing your religious beliefs simply because you didn't have the time or you had other more pressing commitments, you now have an opportunity to reevaluate your position as you begin to plan for the rest of your life. I urge you not to wait until you are on your deathbed to try to reestablish a relationship with your God and religion because fate may intervene and take away the opportunity.

If you are a professed atheist or agnostic, you have probably already gone through the decision process on numerous occasions and feel strongly about your position. I respect your point of view and your right to practice your beliefs. You might want to skip this section on religion and fast-forward to the community issues. All I would ask is that you respect the views of pro-religious people and their right to believe in the importance of religion in their lives. For all seniors who go to church and profess a particular belief, this section will provide you with the opportunity to consider other aspects of your religion in your retirement.

There are a great many seniors who intensify the practice of religion in the latter stages of their lives. Some people believe that religion is more important for older people. The implication is that some seniors may identify a desire to have a stronger commitment to religious beliefs in order to prepare mentally for their eventual passing. The motivation may well be the reality that the closer one is to the end of life, the more important it becomes to look beyond the present and consider issues after death. If religion is the bond that allows you to accept your own mortality and consider the possibility of a life after death, then you can justify your beliefs and commitment to your religion.

There are many other seniors who are strong believers in your religious beliefs because you were born into a particular religion or church and you have never questioned or doubted your commitment.

I personally have always admired people who converted to a particular religion because they made the conscious decision to investigate various alternative religions before they made a commitment to a particular one.

As you plan for retirement you have the opportunity to determine if you have any concerns or doubts about your church and religious commitment and determine if you want to do anything about it. For many, the review might simply reinforce their traditions and personal commitments. For others it might create a desire to make a stronger commitment to their church and religious beliefs.

For most people, your church and religion represents your personal foundation that is a vital part of your life. If you are in this category, you might want to consider how much more you might be able to do in your retirement to fulfill your life's goals.

5. **Community Wants and Needs**—closely allied with your commitment to your church is the issue of your community involvement. As the old adage says, "No man is an island unto themselves." Our community fulfills an important role in our lives since it provides many of the services that are necessary and desirable for our overall well-being.

Most seniors would not be able to live comfortably without the wealth of services and support available in communities across the country. The issue for your retirement planning is to determine what you might want to avail yourself of from the abundance of community services and supports.

The other side of the coin is for you to determine what you might want to do to help other people in your community who may be less fortunate than you are.

You can start by getting a directory from your community governments that details the range of available services. You can use the same directory as a checklist to identify departments or agencies that might need your participation or support.

On the other side of community activities are the non-governmental organizations that provide services, specifically the civic, fraternal and social clubs and organizations in your community. There are literally hundreds of community-based organizations that provide vital services and support to members of their communities. If you look up "social service organizations" in the Yellow Pages© you will find a plethora of organizations that exist to support their communities. The listing can also serve as a checklist to help you determine if you want to avail yourself of any of their services in your retirement.

In addition, you can use the checklist to determine what organizations you might want to get involved in if you are not already involved in community organizations. Every organization in every community in the country needs additional volunteers and financial support. Your retirement provides a wonderful opportunity for you to give back to the community some of your time in partial payment for all the services they have provided for you and your family in the past.

For instance, a local church has been building and supporting Habitat for Humanity homes for over 10 years. There are dedicated seniors who have helped to build over 10 homes for deserving families. Just think about the pride and sense of fulfillment they get when they see the results of their efforts. The families who live in the homes represent an enduring legacy for the seniors who allocated a portion of their time for this noble effort.

There is another group in Atlanta that have dedicated a major amount of their free time to helping multi-handicapped children and adults experience a better quality of social life. Throughout the year they organize social activities like a dance, or picnic or a ballgame, or a trip to the circus. Each summer they take their special-needs friends to the beach for an extended weekend, wheelchairs, crutches and all.

Some of the volunteers became interested in the program because of a sibling or relative who had physical problems but most are ordinary people who simply allocated a large amount of their time to help those who are less fortunate than they are. Think about the wonderful feeling they get at the end of a long, difficult day from helping a totally thankful and smiling handicapped young person?

Another group of senior volunteers spends one night a week at a homeless shelter. They prepare meals and provide support for the homeless, sometimes by giving a haircut or finding clean clothes, or simply being a good listener. If they ever get to bed, it is a cot or the floor. But their motivation is realizing that the homeless are all God's children and like the insightful quotation, "There but for the grace of God, go I." Sometimes we find our calling in strange places.

The point is that every church and community needs volunteers. You have a wonderful opportunity to use your available time; regardless of how little it may be, to help someone in need. The satisfaction and reward will be great. Can you think of a better thing to do than to help your fellow man? That's what fulfillment is all about.

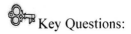 Key Questions:

a. Work:
   ❑ Do you still *need* to work? What is your plan?
   ❑ Do you still *want* to work? What is your plan?

b. Family Relationships:
  ❏ What family relationships do you *want* to improve or maintain?
  ❏ What family relationships do you *need* to improve or maintain?

c. Social Relationships:
  ❏ Do you *need* to or *want* to re-establish or improve any social relationships or friendships?

d. Spiritual:
  ❏ Do you *want or need* to make any changes in your views on spiritual issues or the role of religion in your life?

e. Community:
  ❏ What do you *need* to do within my community that might make a difference for someone less fortunate?
  ❏ What community organizations do you *want* to get involved in?

Chapter 9

Personalized Retirement Plan:
Step #2—Obligations and Commitments

"Life is not the way it's supposed to be. It's the way it is. The way you deal with it is what makes the difference."

~Virginia Satir, Author

The third step in creating your Personalized Retirement Plan is to identify the obligations and commitments that you must consider in structuring your time and activity plan.

All retirees bring "baggage" to retirement. Everyone has unique and personal obligations and commitments that cannot be avoided or left at the doorstep of retirement. Every situation is different but all of the baggage issues need to be reviewed and incorporated into your retirement plan.

The usual sources of obligations and commitments come from some of the following:

- Parents
- Children and grandchildren
- Relatives and friends
- Business or profession
- Organizations and clubs
- Church or synagogue
- Community

Let's take a brief look at each source of potential obligation or commitment to determine if anything needs to be incorporated into you PRP.

- **Parents**—by the time many seniors reach retirement age their parents have already passed away. But sometimes people retire relatively early or their parents live to a ripe old age and there is the possibility of having to care for an aging parent.

Although long life is generally a blessing, sometimes is presents us with a major challenge. There is no "one best solution" for how to care for a dependent parent. All you can do is use good judgment in creating a program that will take care of their needs; while at the same time not overwhelming your own Personalized Retirement Plans.

Fortunately today there are many more options for assisted or independent living. You need to determine what is best for your parent. If the only alternative is for them to live with you, then you will have to find a way to accommodate their needs without forgetting about your own retirement needs and goals.

If your mother or father is able to live independently, and possibly in another city, you need to treat them much like a son or daughter by staying in touch routinely and doing whatever you can to help them, but let them live their own lives until such time they ask or need your direct intervention.

A Personal Story

When I relocated to Atlanta, my mother was residing in an assisted living center in Ohio. Fortunately I had sisters in Ohio would could look after her but mother was very disturbed that her one and only son would be some 500 miles away. As a part of the good-byes I made a promise to her that I would call her regularly and write a personal letter during my weekly travels. She enjoyed the letters very much and it gave me a chance to keep her up to date on our lives in Georgia. Several years later my mother passed away and after the funeral my sisters found a large stack of my letters in her dresser. It turns out that she had saved every letter. They told me that she anxiously awaited the mail every day for my letter. It made me feel proud that I was able to keep my commitment to my mother. Remember: you have only one mother and father and they will love you more than anyone else in your life. We all have an obligation to do whatever it takes to make our parents happy in their later years.

- **Children and Grandchildren**—the most wonderful blessing in life is your children and grandchildren, but they can also represent a major challenge in planning for your retirement, especially if you need to play a direct role in their on-going care or well-being.

We have some close friends who are raising two of their grandsons because their daughter suffered a premature stroke and is incapable of caring for them. Although our friends are in their 70s they are a wonderful role model for love, patience, and perseverance. They never asked why, they simply took over the responsibility of raising their grandsons just as if they were their own children. And they are remarkably young in their attitude and approach to caring for two teenagers.

By the time you reach retirement age your children are most likely on their own, but there is a growing trend for adult children to return to the family nest. It happened to us twice. One of our sons went through a divorce and returned to Atlanta to get his life together and moved into our lower level bedroom. After our son moved out, our single daughter moved in with us to help save money so she could buy her own home. We enjoyed the companionship very much and we were able to have privacy on the first level of our home and our children could retreat to the finished lower level if they wanted to be alone. The point is that you never know what the future holds so you need to be flexible in planning the future.

If any of your adult children have not left the nest, for whatever the reason, or has not been able to break the umbilical cord of dependence, or there is simply an inordinate level of involvement, then you have to determine how you will handle the relationship in retirement. You cannot fail to retire or do the things you want to do in retirement if your children are still directly involved in your daily life. You can't ignore it, you must plan for it.

Sometimes there are situations that can't be avoided. We have five adult children, four sons and a daughter, and five grandsons. Our oldest and youngest sons were born with severe multiple-handicaps. For over 30 years we cared for both of them in our home with the help of our other children and family. Eventually the physical demands became too much for us to handle after our healthy children went off to college and pursued their careers. We made the tough decision to place our special sons into a residential home program that is administered by United Cerebral Palsy. Initially it was very difficult for us to accept that we would not be involved with their care on a daily basis. We fretted and worried that they might not get the same degree of love and protection but that soon melted away as the professional care givers were able to provide them with a similar level of care and personal commitment.

We know hundreds of families who have special needs children. There is a natural reluctance to place these special children in residential homes or institutions but you need to realize that there will come a time when you can no longer care for them in your home due to your age and physical abilities.

There are many millions more parents who have children with less severe challenges. Who knows why a select few families are chosen to carry a special cross during life? All you can do is accept the cross and do your very best to care for your special child even if and when the child becomes a part of your retirement plan.

As a result of our particular family situation, we started the planning process many years before we placed them in the residential program. It is vital that parents in similar situations begin to plan for the day when their special needs children will have to be cared for outside the home. We are still very active in the care and nurturing of our special sons and will continue our involvement until we decease. Then our children and grandchildren will assist with the lifelong responsibility to care for a special relative. We certainly didn't want this kind of lifelong burden but it was not the fault of our special sons. We simply had to accept the responsibility and make the best of the situation. Their needs had to be incorporated into our PRP.

Sometimes life throws you a curve ball and all you can do is accept and respond to it. The important thing is that you not allow your fate to affect the quality of your life. Regardless of the circumstances, you and you planning partner are the master of your own mutual destiny. You can do whatever you need to do to achieve happiness and fulfillment.

- **Relatives and Friends**—the relationship that you enjoy with your relatives and friends is a two-edged sword. One side of the sword provides love, support and endearing relationships. Relatives and friends are the next most important and meaningful relationship in our lives, surpassed only by the relationship with our spouse, or planning partner, and our parents and children. The other side of the sword is that these relationships can also create some of the most serious interpersonal problems and challenges, especially with our relatives.

Everyone has the advantage of being able to choose their friends, but relatives are a result of fate. If a friend disappoints you, you can back away and concentrate on other relationships. But when a relative disappoints, you are stuck with them for life.

There is a line from Shakespeare, "Fate makes for strange bedfellows." We never know what fate will provide in the future. Something might occur that suddenly places a new challenge or obligation in a relationship with a relative or friend. There aren't enough pages to consider all of the unique family and personal situations that could impact your retirement planning. There are some people with few relatives; others have giant clans of relatives. Some people have extremely close relationships with friends, sometimes closer than blood relatives. It is understandable if a relative or friend should have special consideration in a retirement plan. However, keep in mind the planning principle that your retirement is all about you primarily. Don't compromise your life unless it is something that you really want to do.

If you enjoy wonderful friends, you should continue to nurture the relationship and plan on spending as much time as you can with them in your retirement years. Your closest friends are your greatest treasures, especially those friendships that have endured for many years.

Everyone needs to have a few very close friends and possibly one "best friend." These are the people who can provide us with advice and counsel, usually better than our relatives can because a friend tends to be more objective.

Similarly, most of us have favorite relatives and we all seem to have some relatives that we are not particularly close to. That's okay because there is no rule that states you must get along with everybody. You have the right to pick and choose your friends and determine which relatives you want to remain close to. Don't let blood get in the way of common sense.

When some retirees decide to move to a retirement area, they need to recognize that they could be leaving the comfort and security of many good and loyal friends. Although every retirement community advertises how great the people are in their community, the reality is that you will have to develop brand new friendships. The older you get, the more difficult it is for you to develop new friends. If you have a difficult time making new friends, you need to reconsider your relocation plans or find some way to stay in closer touch with your current best friends.

One idea to consider is to let your planning partner and family know the names of your best friends and relatives, if it is not already known. Some day your family and friends will be helping the surviving partner plan your funeral. One exercise that is covered in a later chapter suggests that you draft a list of the people you want to be involved in your funeral either as eulogists or pallbearers. This will cause you to think about who are really your best friends and relatives.

- **Business and Career Relationships**—beyond the personal relationships, some retirees will need to consider the impact of various business and professional relationships in their retirement planning.

For instance, there are literally thousands of family-owned businesses that create some unique challenges in retirement. I know one family who has owned a very successful restaurant business and they have been able to pass the torch from one generation to another rather successfully. But the business is so much a part of the family that none of the family members could ever withdraw totally from involvement in the restaurant. It's literally in their blood and provides them with a major source of pride, income and family heritage.

If you are involved in a similar situation, you need to determine how you plan to extract yourself from the business so that you are actually able to retire. You might be involved with a business or career group that will require some type of on-going participation during your retirement. Whatever the relationship, you need to determine your role and level of participation to insure that you are able to really break away enough to actually retire. I don't imply that you must abandon the relationship; rather you need to determine your role and amount of participation if you have a business or profession that will require some of your time into the future.

Another source of great friendships is the co-workers or customers or clients that we developed relationships with over many years. Some relationships may have blossomed into dear, close friendships. If you have relationships that could cause you to be involved in on-going activities, then you need to factor them into your retirement plan.

One of my very best friends was a former client. Although many professional firms frown on getting too close to clients, sometimes you meet an individual who you want to become friends with. We shared the same birthday and had many things in common. Our friendship grew and eventually our spouses joined the friendship and we did many things together, including some great golfing trips around the country. However, we were very discreet in our relationship and never let our personal feelings get in the way of important business decisions. In fact, few people in either company knew that we were close personal friends. When we both retired, we were able to bring our relationship out in the open and not worry about any potential conflicts of interest. My friend developed a brain tumor and fought the good fight but succumbed to the dread disease. I was honored to be one of two eulogists as the funeral. His wife will always be a dear personal friend. Good friends are a treasure.

There is another important consideration with business or career friendships. In some instances, the friendship is one-sided in that your planning partner may not know the individual or have as close a relationship. If you plan to bring these one-sided friends into your retirement plans, it is important that your planning partner is involved and agrees that the relationship can be truly mutual.

- **Organizations and Clubs**—some people get really involved with organizations and clubs whether social, civic, fraternal, charitable, professional, educational or governmental, sometimes to a fault. If a major portion of your time in recent years has gone into activities in a club or organization, you absolutely must take this into consideration in your retirement planning, especially if you intend to have on-going responsibilities in the organization.

Another friend became very involved with the Boy Scouts. Although it was a tremendous and noble activity that benefited many thousands of boys, and provided him with a great sense of accomplishment, he got to the point where it consumed his time almost to the exclusion of everything else, much like an addiction.

I have another friend who is "married" to his country club. You can find him there just about every waking moment. Whether it is golf, or gin, or cribbage, or poker, or swimming, or dining or just hanging out with the boys, my friend has made his club the focal point in his life. Some people might suggest that that he needs "to get a life" but that is a decision that he and his partner need to discuss during their retirement planning.

The challenge in both of these examples deals with the mutuality of retirement planning. This one-sided addition to an activity is usually only gratifying to the individual. If you spend excessive time on an activity, regardless of how rewarding it may be to you, it takes away from the quality time you could be spending with your significant other. But, if both partners are involved in your own personal activity and that is what each of you wants, then it is up to the two of you to decide how you want to spend your time. The danger comes when one partner excludes the other from their most meaningful activities.

Another challenge involves some seniors who are involved in a large number of organizations and clubs and use the activities as an excuse not to be involved with their partner. This is a dangerous situation that can lead to a stressful relationship, arguments and sometimes divorce. If you are a "groupie" and feel a need to be involved in lots of things, that's okay, as long as your partner is comfortable with your program.

- **Church and Spiritual**—the role of religion is an important consideration throughout your entire life, not simply when you are growing old. The key issue is that you need to determine if you will have any on-going obligations or commitments in your church or spiritually as you enter retirement that might impact what you do or where you want to live or how you will conduct your remaining years.
I know a person who is a founding member of a Christian church in our neighborhood. He is extremely proud that his name is on the plaque in front of church that identifies him as a founding

member. It is highly unlikely that he will ever be able to leave that church as a result of his close personal commitment and level of participation.

We also have friends who are strict Orthodox Jews. They now live in a larger city that has an Orthodox synagogue. If they were to consider moving to another smaller community, their choices of where to live might be somewhat restricted because most Orthodox synagogues are located in larger cities.

In our personal situation, my wife tries very hard to attend mass on a daily basis. As a result, it is important for us to be located relatively close to a Catholic church to reduce the daily travel time.

Many seniors develop a new sense of commitment to their religion and spirituality as a result of having more time in their retirement years to devote to the renewal of their faith. It is also generally true that a great many seniors spend more time in church in their later years than in their younger years. If you desire to be more active in your church or religion, it needs to be considered in your PRP.

- **Community**—the last consideration in recognizing your obligations and commitments is to review your current or desired roles or responsibilities in your community or various levels of government or politics.

Every community, city, county and state needs good, qualified people to help deal with the problems of growth and the changing times. If you are not currently involved, it might be something you want to add to your wish list.

We have a friend in Ohio who was asked to run for a seat on his local school board after his retirement. He was reluctant since he had no prior school or political experience, but he had decades of practical experience in managing a successful business. Apparently the voters saw the connection between his career skills and the needs on the school board because he was elected on his first try. Not only is he making a wonderful contribution of his time and talent to a critical community need, he is also enjoying it immensely.

If you are an active participant in community or political activities and desire to stay involved, it is something that needs to be incorporated into your RPG. Your decision could have significant impact on where you decide to live in your retirement years since most communities and political organizations are run by long time local people.

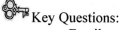Key Questions:
  a. Family
     ❑ Do you have obligations or commitments with parents, children or grandchildren that will influence your retirement plan?
     ❑ How will you deal with these issues when you can no longer fulfill your obligation?

  b. Friends and Relatives:
     ❑ Do you have obligations or commitments to friends or relatives that will impact your retirement plans?
     ❑ Who are the friends and relatives that you want to stay close to during retirement?

  c. Business and Professional Relationships:
     ❑ Do you have on-going business or professional obligations or commitments to consider that will influence your retirement plan?

     ❑ Are there any business or professional relationships or friendships that need to be addressed?

 f. Organizations:

     ❑ Do you have any obligations, commitments or preferences involving social or civic organizations or clubs that will affect your retirement plan?

     ❑ Have you considered your partner when evaluating your obligations and commitments to these organizations and clubs?

 g. Church and Religion Relationships:

     ❑ Are there obligations or commitments that involve your church or religion that might affect your retirement plan?

 h. Community Relationships:

     ❑ Do you have community or political obligations, commitments or desires that you need to consider in developing your retirement plan?

All of us have unique obligations and commitments that must be considered when developing our retirement plan. The important thing is to be open, honest and up front about each obligation and commitment while remembering that your retirement plan is in your hands. You will ultimately have to make some tough choices between what you want to do and what you need to do.

Chapter 10

Personalized Retirement Plan:
Step #3—Personal Inventory

"Build upon strengths, and weaknesses will gradually take care of themselves."
> ~*Joyce C. Lock, Poet*

Everybody is good at something. That special something usually has to do with your occupation or career. If you were a high school football coach, your strengths were likely to be organization, leadership, motivation, discipline and perseverance. In short, you had a real strength in working with people to accomplish a common goal.

A great many retirees leave their jobs and careers and eventually begin to look around for things to do that are compatible with their interests and skills. This chapter suggests that one of the best ways to find happiness, and sometimes additional income, in retirement is to use your strengths for your personal benefit.

The challenge is to identify what it is that you are really good at. You need to start by taking a personal inventory of your strengths. Along the way you also want to look at the other side of the coin and identify your weaknesses or those things that you're not particularly good at.

There are also some retirees who simply had "jobs" in their careers that might not have been what they really wanted to do or were particularly good at doing. For instance, the children of business owners or professionals tend to go into the family business or pursue a career similar to that of their parents. One friend of mine became a CPA and went to work in his father's firm only to find out years later that he actually did not like being an accountant. When he retired, he embarked on an entirely new career in personal counseling that he was really good at and looked forward to doing.

You will be asked to conduct a personal exercise to determine your strengths, weaknesses, opportunities and threats (commonly referred to as a SWOT analysis). Each partner should do their analysis separately. When completed, the analysis should be shared with the partner and possibly other trusted family members, friends, or advisors to validate the results. The intent is to ensure that you have captured the essence of your true strengths and weaknesses. Sometimes we are a little biased about what we are really good or poor at. Your partner will either confirm or question your analysis. That's okay because it will lead to important dialog and eventually to a more accurate picture of your strengths and weaknesses.

Those of you who have a business or corporate background have probably used the SWOT concept. It is a tool used by organizations to plan more effectively by analyzing each of the components of their business, namely their strengths, weaknesses, opportunities, and threats. The technique is credited to Albert Humphrey, who led a research project at Stanford University in the 1960s and 1970s using data from the Fortune 500 companies.

It is my contention that to be happy in retirement you need to get involved in things you really want to do and that you do well, whether you do it for fun or to earn additional income. The implication is that you will get more satisfaction and results from doing something that comes easy to you than doing something that causes you to struggle. The place to start is to conduct a SWOT analysis that will help you take an inventory of your overall capabilities.

S.W.O.T. Analysis

The term "SWOT" stands for Strengths, Weaknesses, Opportunities and Threats. The SWOT model is highly applicable as a foundation for retirement planning. You should make a list of your strengths, weaknesses, opportunities and threats. Then review them with your spouse, significant other or a friend, to verify your findings.

❑ **Strengths**—your strengths are those things that you or your partner are really good at. You should use your strengths to guide what you might want to do relative to your current career or a potential new career. For example, let's say that both of you are particularly good at entertaining. You enjoy it and people enjoy having you do it. One option for your retirement might be to work in a restaurant or start a Bed & Breakfast Inn that allows you to utilize your strengths.

It is important to determine if you are better at working with people or working with things. Are you out-going, happy, and carefree or are you inward and introverted? Keep in mind that there is no one best set of strengths or qualities. They are what they are. Your job is to recognize and accept what they are. It is not likely that you will be able to make any dramatic changes in your personality. You need to find a way to make the most with what you have.

The key is to pattern what you do in retirement with your strengths, capabilities and core competencies.

For instance, doctors and nurses devote their lives to caring for people. Their over-riding personal strength is their compassion for their fellow man. This is what drove their career and they would probably find satisfaction and fulfillment in retirement if they devoted a portion of their time to activities that capitalized on their instinctive quality of compassion.

❑ **Weaknesses**—your weaknesses imply that you should avoid doing things that you are not good at. For instance, if you are not good at sports, you might want to put a lesser priority on the importance of golf and tennis and tackle things that you are good at. If you have talent for painting and love golf, a good compromise is to paint things that involve golf. The concept is to capitalize on your strengths and minimize your weaknesses.

A more positive way to address weaknesses is to think of them as "challenges." It is true that not everyone is perfect. We all have our challenges. It is important to identify the things that we need to improve so that we don't inadvertently get involved in things that we are not very good at. Also, retirement provides an opportunity to work on our shortcomings and improve the quality of our interpersonal relationships with our partner, family, friends and associates.

Sometimes partners or those close to us are better able to identify our weaknesses or deficiencies if we are willing to listen and accept their point of view.

❑ **Opportunities**—your opportunities represent all those things that you might want to do but held back doing for various reasons, most of which might not be applicable in retirement. For instance, if you are a complete nut about physical conditioning, you might want to explore how you can turn your interest into a retirement opportunity.

Opportunities are much like the weather, they come and go. There are two important considerations about opportunities. First, you have to recognize an opportunity when you see it. Second, you have to take advantage of the opportunity before it fades away.

The first step in recognizing an opportunity is to understand what you should be looking for. The purpose for determining your opportunities in retirement is to create awareness about what to look for. For instance, if you have a huge desire to travel and see the world, but lack adequate finances, then you have to keep your eye open for ways to see the world without spending a lot of money. As an example, you could get a job on a cruise ship and see the world while still earning extra income.

The second requirement for being opportunistic is to latch onto an opportunity when you see it. Most people are better at identifying opportunities than they are at grabbing hold of them.

There are literally countless opportunities for retirees to get involved in wonderfully interesting, exciting, and rewarding activities, whether as a volunteer or to earn additional money. Just about every organization in the country is actively seeking volunteers. There are many senior-friendly organizations that provide advice and counsel on how to get involved in whatever activity that tickles your fancy.

There are two groups that do an exceptional job of providing information for seniors who are interested in either second careers or volunteering.

- American Association of Retired Persons (AARP)—go to www.aarp.org
- National and Community Service, the Senior Corps—go to www.seniorcorps.gov

Instead of listing hundreds of other organizations, you can search the Internet by entering "senior organizations" or "retiree organizations" or any particular area of interest you might have like "senior part-time employment".

❑ **Threats**—your threats are those real or perceived negatives that could rear up and threaten your retirement unless you plan around them. For instance, if your retirement nest egg is limited or might not adequately support your preferred lifestyle, you could face the threat of running out of money and the necessity of working longer than anticipated or continuing to work on a part-time basis. Therefore, your Personalized Retirement Plan must address how you should bolster this threat to your nest egg by exploring full or part-time work or the creation of a business venture to generate additional income.

Threats come in many sizes and shapes. You might identify threats to your income or investments; health issues; economic issues; global issues; or a myriad of smaller threats dealing with your home or hobbies or interests. For instance, a friend in Ohio spent an inordinate amount of time at his country club playing golf and cards. In his way of thinking, he had an ideal retirement. Then one day his plans were upset when the club advised that they could no longer make it financially and were going to shut down. Suddenly his world was threatened and had to make new plans to ensure his psychological wellbeing.

The identification of potential threats is the same as making contingency plans. You ask a whole series of questions that start with, "What if...?" But don't become so involved in trying to anticipate all the potential problems that you forget to have fun. You need to focus on the major issues like income and health.

Be sure to allow each other to express your feelings openly and honestly. The purpose is not to start a heated discussion or open old wounds, rather it is to provide the forum for you and your partner to get some issues on the table that might stand in the way of creating the right environment for retirement.

Both partners need to be sensitive to the other person's point of view and expect that you might not necessarily agree with each other's assessment. None the less, you need to go through this exercise because some of the issues you uncover might be standing in the way of creating a truly open and honest relationship.

For instance, there are lots of couples and single persons who have a very difficult challenge when they try to live within their financial means, a problem that could have disastrous consequences in retirement. Sometimes it is one partner who has the problem, sometimes it is both. If this problem is identified in your planning session as a weakness, you have the obligation to do something about it rather than remain silent and sweep it under the carpet.

Another example comes to mind about a couple that had a conflict over where they wanted to live in their retirement. One partner tended to resist change and preferred to stay in their comfortable homestead where they had lived for 40 years, close to their children and extended family. One partner loved the security that came from tradition and well ingrained habit patterns. The other partner was more open and expansive and desperately wanted to break free from a family-dominated environment that was perceived as being oppressive and boring. This partner wanted to move to the Sunbelt and get away from the harsh winters and the family scene, something the other partner just did not understand.

If this kind of issue is not resolved, it is fair to say that this couple's retirement could be forever strained and probably cause them to drift apart, not necessarily into divorce but into a state of emotional and physical separation.

Perhaps the classic example is the problem that many retired people experience when the primary wage earner retires and becomes a homebound retiree. Inevitably, the new retiree unintentionally gets in the way of the other partner. Suddenly the retired partner begins to question and critique how things are done around the house. Although they mean well, it is bound to lead to some serious confrontations.

If both partners had discussed their feelings about retirement, they could probably avoid the problem. There is nothing wrong with one partner spending more time at home as long as they recognize the prerogatives of the other partner. You need to remember that somehow, some way, your partner was able to manage the home without any of your help for several decades and they don't want or need any unsolicited advice and counsel, thank you very much.

If you go into retirement without a plan and mope around the house all day because you have nothing better to do then you are bound to get in the way and criticize everything you see. If you have a partner like this, you really need to start your formal PRP before the problem boils over into a major crisis.

Core Competencies

After you have completed your SWOT analysis, you need to take some additional time and focus more intensely on your strengths, or the things that you do really well. Usually your strengths are things that differentiate you from your partner or other family members, relatives, and friends. For instance, some people are blessed with the ability to communicate really well while others have a difficult time standing up in front of an audience. Most people have more than one strength but usually there is one particular strength that stands out and represents a person's *core competency.*

For instance, when Ted Williams was a fighter pilot during World War II, it was reported that he had eyes like one in several million people. During training exercises the pilots would take target practice by shooting at a large cloth target attached to the back of another plane. Ted allegedly could count the bullet holes in the flying target from several hundred yards away before landing. Is it no wonder that he was able to see a 90 mph fast ball or the action on a slider or curve? His eyesight was his core competency.

A person's core competency may not be obvious; you have to dig down underneath the surface of a strength to identify the skill or capability that allows the person to excel at something.

If you watch professional athletes, whether it is baseball, football, soccer, tennis, golf, etc., you might at first think that their core competency had something to do with their particular skills as a good hitter or kicker or runner, etc. But when you look at the underlying core competency, it is more likely to be their extremely fine-tuned hand and eye coordination that allows them to excel at what they do. That is why good athletes tend to be very good at other sports that require similar skills. For instance, what average club tennis player could return a 140 m.p.h. serve from a world class player? Yet the professionals return these thunderous serves routinely because of their highly tuned hand and eye coordination.

A Closer Look at Core Competencies

An accountant's core competency is not necessarily their knowledge of accounting rules and regulations. It is more likely to be their analytical skills.

An attorney's core competency is not necessarily their knowledge of the law. It is probably their ability to discern between right and wrong.

A professor's core competency is not necessarily their extreme knowledge of their specialty. It is more likely to be their ability to impart knowledge.

A surgeon's core competency is not necessarily their knowledge of the human body. It is more likely to be their ability to diagnose and solve a medical problem.

A mother or father's core competency is not necessarily rearing children. It is more likely to be their ability to understand the needs of their children.

In management consulting, the core competency is not necessarily a detailed knowledge of a particular industry or activity, although that is very important. Rather it is probably the ability of the consultant to analyze and solve problems, and importantly to bring along the client so they understand and are willing to adopt the recommended solution.

Finally, an architect's core competency is not necessarily their skills in designing buildings and structures. It is more likely to be their ability to envision something three-dimensionally that does not now exist.

Key Point: everybody has a core competency, but you might never have taken the time to figure out what it is.

Here are more examples about how your inner strengths might point a direction for retirement activities that you might be well qualified to do because of your innate core competency.

A retired salesman or teacher should have a much better probability of success by doing something that involves working with people.

A retired policeman or fireman or soldier might consider doing something that involves the protection of people and things.

A retired contractor would probably be good at helping people plan and build things.

A retired engineer would probably be good at helping people fix things.

A retired financial executive would probably be good at helping people organize things. And so on.

Now that you understand the concept of a core competency, you should look at what you did in your career and boil your strengths down to its root skill or underlying core competency.

Once you understand your core competency you will be better able to identify the kind of things that you could do in retirement that have a better chance at doing as well as the potential for you to achieve a higher level of satisfaction and fulfillment.

Key Questions:

- What are your strengths?
- What is your greatest strength or your underlying core competency?
- What are your weaknesses?
- What opportunities are there that you want to capitalize on?
- Are there issues or threats that need to be resolved or avoided?

Chapter 11

Retirement Plan:
Step #4: Life after Retirement

"The greatest discovery of my generation is that human beings can alter their lives by altering their attitudes of mind."
~William James

This chapter is about helping you adjust to the psychological aspects of "life after retirement". The intent is to provide you with an early warning that you <u>might</u> possibly experience a difficult adjustment period in the early days and months after you retire. It may be a confusing time if you thought that retirement was going to be a totally happy experience. If you are one of the many retirees that experience this condition, don't worry, it is a normal reaction to the loss of something you have been involved in for many decades, namely your job and career.

The fact is that it is not easy to walk away from something you have been doing for many years. You will miss the people, your colleagues, your customers or patients or clients or students or commuter friends, etc. You will also miss the routine that you followed every day of your working life. Eventually you will also miss the feeling of wellbeing and importance that your job and career provided, whether it was your rank, title, or perks. You quickly learn that in retirement you have none of the trappings of your former life. When it all suddenly comes to an end, you may feel a sense of loss that only a fellow retiree will be able to understand and identify with.

The key to lessening the impact of this post-retirement condition is to get involved in something that helps you to replace the sense of wellbeing that your job and career provided. For some retirees, the adjustment is more difficult. They evolve into an intensive depression that saps their physical and emotional strength.

If you were a "stay at home Mom or Dad", your world will be turned upside down when your partner is suddenly camped out in your private domain and attempts to help you in your daily routine and inadvertently and unintentionally gets in your way. Many a spouse has been driven to the edge of sanity by a retired partner who upsets the normal schedule of a household by their retired presence.

The adjustment process in retirement is similar to other major changes in your life. Try to recall your feelings when your youngest child went off to pre-school or kindergarten. You cried and fretted all day long as you empathized about abandoning your helpless little baby. Another emotional touch point was when that same child, now a teenager goes off to college. You know for sure that life will never be the same without them, and you are right. A few years later you watch pensively as your grown-up son or daughter gets married. Your life is now totally turned upside down. How can you ever survive without children in the house? When will things ever be normal again? The reality is that things never will be like they were. You simply have to adjust and get on with life.

So it is with retirement, in spite of your feelings, life goes on. But, it is important that you anticipate that you may have some downer days in the early stages of retirement. That's okay; you will have plenty of company. You can get over it faster by filling your days with things that you planned in advance to do that you really enjoy.

Accepting Who You Are

There is another issue that surfaces for many retirees. It deals with aging and the eventual reality that you are entering the last quarter of your life. Regardless of how you feel about growing old, there is nothing you can do to stop the process. But you can be very proactive in taking good care of your mind and body to lessen the impact of aging. The fact is that today is as young as you will be the rest of your life.

An old saying goes, "You are only as old as you feel." The fact is that your attitude has a lot to do with how you feel about getting older. If you think you have aches and pains, you will have aches and pains. If you don't let yourself become disheartened by the aging process, you will feel and act like a much younger person. You can control how you feel and act. It amounts to mind over matter.

One of the key issues in retirement is attitude. There will be lots of things that a person can't plan for in retirement but the one thing everyone has the power to create and maintain is a positive attitude.

Types of Retirees

There are two types of seniors that arrive at the gate to retirement, regardless of age. The first are the seniors who can hardly wait to retire; namely, **The Anxious.** They have been thinking about retirement for years, literally counting the days. These are the type who rush out and buy a motor home and hit the road the day after they retire. But sadly the euphoria may not last overly long. Much of their retirement thought process was based on intuitive instincts and may not have been something that was arrived at after careful thought or discussion with their partner.

For instance, I read an article in the newspaper about an auto mechanic who won several million dollars in a state lottery. He immediately quit his job and announced that he was moving to a lake community where he would buy a boat and spend the rest of his life fishing for bass. I often wondered what his spouse thought about his plan, especially if she wasn't too excited about fishing. In this instance, there might have been a deep psychological issue grinding away in the inner feelings of the spouse that might eventually erupt and catch the other partner by complete surprise.

A similar situation might occur if one partner has been the dominant person in the relationship and tended to make most of the important decisions with little or no input from the other partner. Either the submissive partner continues to be submissive or the issue needs to get out on the table for discussion. Here again the dominant partner might not even be aware that there is a problem. The usual response is something like, "What do you mean I have made all the important decisions? I always asked but you never had an opinion. I've worked very hard to provide for all of us and I'm offended that you aren't happy with the way I've done things, etc. etc."

The cold, hard reality of retirement is that two spouses are positioned to spend a whole lot more time together and there is a categorical need to make sure that you identify any issues that could lead to conflict or possibly even separation or divorce.

It is significant to note that the rate of divorce increases at two critical points in the marriage cycle. First, when the couple becomes "empty nesters" and they suddenly realize that it was the commitment to their children that had been keeping them together. One or both partners wake up one morning and determine that they no longer have much in common with the person they have shared a bed with for 25 or more years.

The second critical time for potential divorce is in the early years of retirement. Suddenly the spouses are thrust together during the day when one or both had previously been involved in their career. They literally get in each other's way and start to criticize the housekeeping, or menu, or daily habits, or any of a thousand things. That leads to arguments and fights and eventually complete disharmony. In many instances the immediate family and close friends are dismayed because they thought the couple was happily married.

Key Point: the planning and implementation of a retirement plan must be a mutual endeavor. Both partners must participate and express their points of view in an open, frank, and honest manner. If either or both partners are not able to communicate, they will only drift further apart during retirement.

The Second Thoughters

The second category of retiree is those that arrive kicking and screaming at the retirement gate but they aren't sure if they really want to retire or if they have enough money or if they care about it one way or the other. They are more likely to have second thoughts about retirement. Some of them may have been "forced" to take mandatory retirement due to age or seniority.

For instance, some airlines in the past had a mandatory retirement age for pilots. One of my friends retired as a senior captain at age 60 and immediately went back to work as a corporate pilot because he just wasn't ready to give up flying. The point is that there are many seniors who are not ready psychologically or emotionally or financially to retire at a pre-determined age.

A 25 year old thinks a 50 year old person is ancient. But life has a way of changing your attitude about age the older you get. You realize that 50 is not very old and can't remember why you used to think it was. Ironically you will learn that you can have the same feelings at 60 and 70 and even 80. The point is that if you think you are still young, and you act like you are young, then you are young, at least in your mind and that is the most important consideration.

Many seniors arrive at age 50 or 60 or 70 and discover that they like their lifestyle, including their job and their activities. The idea that you should suddenly abandon your job or career is distasteful. If you are in this group, it is important for you to go through this planning exercise for two reasons. First, you need to examine the pros and cons of retirement in a more thoughtful manner. Second, your actions should always incorporate the thoughts and wishes of your partner. Although one partner might not be ready to retire, it is possible that the other partner desperately needs a change in lifestyle. Some form of partial retirement might be an option.

If you want to continue working beyond the normal retirement age, whether by desire or need, then you should incorporate that in your PRP. Just make sure both partners arrive at the decision mutually.

Keep in mind that our society and culture has placed an arbitrary age expectation on retirement. For many years the federal government felt that retirement should start at age 65. More recently the Social Security entry age was increased to 67. Some companies have arbitrary age or seniority guidelines. There is nothing magical about being 50 or 60 or 65 or 70. It is simply a point in time. You and only you are able to determine at what point you want to retire, even if you choose not to retire at all.

For instance, my grandfather had several careers and never stopped working full time. He suffered a heart attack at his office when he was 85 years old. The mere thought of not working and being productive was totally foreign to his way of thinking. I also think his longevity and mental acuity was partially attributed to his work ethic. He believed that work was an integral part of life.

Those who run eagerly into retirement may not understand people like my grandfather but the wonderful thing about life is that everybody has the opportunity to determine their own destiny.

Below is a summary of key questions you need to discuss after reading this chapter.

Key Questions:

- Are both of you psychologically, emotionally and financially ready for retirement?
- What is your attitude about retirement? Your partner?
- Do you have enough money to retire or will you need to continue working full or part-time?
- Is retirement your decision or is it being imposed on you?
- Will you be able to cope with the loss of career and the recognition and rewards you got from it?
- How do you plan to replace the satisfaction, recognition and feeling of self-worth that you career provided?
- Do you want to stop or merely slow down?
- Are there alternatives to retirement? A new career? Something you've always wanted to do?

Chapter 12

Personalized Retirement Plan:
Step #5—Life Goals and Fulfillment

"Occasionally in life there are those moments of unutterable fulfillment which cannot be completely explained by those symbols called words. Their meanings can only be articulated by the inaudible language of the heart."

~Dr. Martin Luther King, Jr.

Psychologists tell us that the highest level of achievement in life is to arrive at a condition called "self-fulfillment" or "self-actualization." This is a condition in which a person feels gratified about what they have done or accomplished in their career and life.

The problem that many of us face is that we have not formalized or verbalized our personal fulfillment objective. Ask yourself the question, "What would cause you to feel that your life has been fulfilled?"

Keep in mind that fulfillment is a highly personal combination of accomplishments and conditions that are totally unique to each individual. The challenge in retirement is to understand what you have done in your attempt to achieve personal fulfillment and what you still need to accomplish. The key is to identify your unique set of goals and write them down so you can achieve fulfillment before you pass to the Great Beyond.

You must recognize that fulfillment is not one particular thing that you have accomplished in your life, rather it is an accumulation of many things or sets of conditions that when added up provides you with a sense of comfort and satisfaction. You could say it is a "body of work" that you have been involved in all your life. The feeling of fulfillment is something that usually happens toward the end of your life because it usually takes a lifetime of activity to meet your fulfillment goals.

When you were young you could experience happiness as you accomplished something meaningful, like a promotion or the birth of a child, but it is unlikely you got a feeling of complete satisfaction or fulfillment. There is always another hill to climb, another goal to strive for, and another something that needs doing. It is the repeated accomplishments on a broad front of initiatives that can eventually result in a sense of fulfillment.

If one of your career goals was to become the top person in your company or institution or profession and you were able to accomplish your goal, the achievement provides a sense of satisfaction that can ultimately result in fulfillment if and when you are able to use the achievement as a springboard for doing something meaningful and beneficial for you, your family and others.

For instance, I have a very close friend who was able to achieve remarkable success in his business career. Although he was quite satisfied with his success, he didn't feel truly fulfilled until he was able to use his wealth to build and fund several orphanages in depressed countries around the world. He then was able to feel a wonderful sense of fulfillment that will now serve as his legacy in the minds and hearts of all of the thousands of orphans and homeless people who have benefited from his success and charity.

This example doesn't mean that you have to do something large and noble like my friend did, it simply illustrates the concept of fulfillment. You can achieve a sense of complete fulfillment by achieving the primary goals in your life. It may have nothing to do with fame or fortune. It has everything to do with setting goals and doing your best to achieve them.

For instance, a stay-at-home mother can achieve a beautiful form of personal fulfillment by reflecting on the success of her children. My mother felt like a million bucks when she saw me walk up on stage and receive my college diploma, something she was not able to do. The diploma was simply a symbol of the many, many things she did throughout my growing up years that made it possible for me to go to college and earn a degree.

Fulfillment and Legacy

"If we truly want to create a life that is grounded in basic well-being, we must decide to commit ourselves to learning what it takes to thrive instead of merely survive."   ~Susan Velasquez, Author

For most people the achievement of their fulfillment goals represents their contribution to the creation of their personal legacy. Our legacy is something that serves as a constant reminder of our presence here on earth long after we are gone.

For instance, many buildings and bridges and roads of the world have people's names inscribed on them. In one way or another, the name on the edifice represents a form of legacy. The philanthropist whose donation built the edifice intended the money to be used for some noble purpose, whether a school or art gallery or park, etc., but for those who use the edifice or structure, it represents an insight into the legacy the donor wanted to be remembered by.

One classic example is Alfred Nobel. The following was found on the Nobel Website...

"In 1867 Alfred Nobel obtained a patent on a special type of nitroglycerine which he called "dynamite." The invention quickly proved its usefulness in building and construction. Alfred Nobel wound up with a total of 355 patents, some more imaginative than useful, others both extremely practicable and valuable. He went on experimenting in pursuit of inventions in many fields, notably with synthetic materials. Income from the many enterprises all over the world in which he had interests made him one of the wealthiest men in Europe."

"In January 1897 it was learned that he had left the bulk of his considerable estate to a fund, the interest on which was to be awarded annually to the persons whose work had been of the greatest benefit to mankind. The statutes of the foundation which administered the fund - the Nobel Foundation - were adopted on 29 June 1900."

And thus, the Nobel Peace Prize was born. It is rather remarkable that one of the most prestigious awards in the world would become the legacy of the man who invented a product that was both useful as well as destructive.

Since most of us will not have our fulfillment goals memorialized like Alfred Nobel, it is none the less important that we define our desired legacy so that it will provide us with the guidelines to use in creating our fulfillment goals.

The next questions that you and your partner need to answer are:

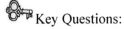 Key Questions:

- What are the primary accomplishments in your career and life?
- What personal goals did you establish for yourself?
- If you didn't have specific goals, describe the condition or set of circumstances that will make you feel happy and content in retirement.
- What personal goals do you still want to accomplish in retirement?
- What will provide you with a true sense of satisfaction and personal fulfillment?
- What would you like your legacy to be? How do you want to be remembered?

Chapter 13

Personalized Retirement Plan:
Step #6—Physical Conditioning

"You have to stay in shape. My grandmother, she started walking five miles a day when she was 60. She's 97 today and we don't know where the hell she is. " ~Ellen DeGeneres

Most of us have done things in our lives that might have been bad for our health and longevity. Think about the late nights, the skipped meals, the lack of exercise, the days away from home, the stress, both real and imagined. Then there were times when we ate too much, including lots of high calorie stuff, or drank too much or smoked a little or a lot or tried to show our skills at company picnics only to end up with a bad back or sprained ankle. Occasionally we would get serious about our physical condition and go on an exercise program or a diet or some other temporary healthful way of life. We've all been there, done that, and maybe still are. The point is that good physical health is something that we have to work on our entire lives. It doesn't come easy; we have to work at it all the time.

The reality is that we end up somehow, someway on the doorstep of retirement with the body that we helped to mold, whether we like it or not. But if you want to enjoy retirement for any extended period of time, you need to do whatever you can to preserve what you got or perhaps improve as best you can one or more parts of your physical health. It begins with being honest with yourself about your true physical condition.

One of the major causes of health problems is weight, specifically obesity. Currently, more than 64% of U.S. adults are either overweight or obese (National Health and Nutrition Examination Survey). This figure represents a 14% increase in the prevalence rate from ten years prior and a 36% increase in the past 20 years. The statistics are shocking:

- 58 million adults are overweight; 40 million obese; 3 million morbidly obese
- 78% of adults not meeting basic activity level recommendations
- 25% completely sedentary
- 76% increase in Type II diabetes in adults since 1990

Taking care of your body becomes more important in retirement because there is a direct cause and effect relationship between how well you care for your body and your longevity. In a nutshell, if you want to live longer, you must take care of your body.

The next step in creating your PRP is to conduct a personal inventory to determine your true physical wants and needs. The desire is to start fresh and take an honest reading on your exact condition, not who you were years ago or who you would like to be, but who you are now.

Physical Examination

If your last physical is over a year old, it is highly recommended that you have a complete physical examination from your personal physician. It is vital that you understand the condition of your body because it will directly affect your retirement planning. Also keep in mind that your body is much like a fine wine, it will age well if you take care of it. If you need to lose a few pounds, or perhaps more, it is safe to say that your physical condition will directly affect your life expectancy in retirement. The intent is to take an inventory of your present condition and then determine what you might need to do to help ensure a longer and healthier life expectancy in retirement.

One technique you should consider is to create a simple chart of your **key physical indicators** (KPI) to serve as a personal "dashboard" to monitor your physical condition. The dashboard in your car provides you with a quick indicator of speed, mileage, temperature, oil pressure and gas consumption. Similarly, there are a handful of physical measurements that can provide you with a quick indication of your physical wellbeing. Below is a sample KPI that you can use as a starting point for assessing your physical condition.

Key Physical Indicators	Actual	Target	Goal
❏ Weight			
❏ Weight/height ratio			
❏ Blood Pressure			
❏ Pulse			
▪ Normal			
▪ Exercise			
❏ Cholesterol			
▪ Total			
▪ LDL (bad)			
▪ Triglyceride (fat)			
▪ HDL (good)			
❏ Blood sugar			
❏ Prostate Specific Antigen (PSA) for men			
❏ Calcium			

You should meet with your doctor and develop the measurements to post on your personal KPI chart. The "actual" numbers would come from your latest physical results. The "target" numbers would be determined by you and your doctor and the generally accepted range for each indicator based on your age, overall condition and your personal goals. If there are other measurements that might be important to you, just add them to the chart.

The key physical indicators can serve as the starting point for determining what actions or activities you need to initiate that will control or improve your dashboard numbers.

For instance, if you have a blood pressure problem, it might be brought under control by weight loss or exercise, usually in some combination. Whatever the issue, you should use your retirement planning session as the catalyst to create a plan of action for each indicator that you need or want to improve.

Your physical improvement plan may require that you make some serious adjustments in your lifestyle. All of the excuses that you may have used in the past for not eating well or not exercising regularly are no longer valid. Retirement provides you with the opportunity to create a new lifestyle, especially in eating well and getting involved in a regular exercise program.

The Wellness Concept

An approach to healthy living that is growing in popularity is the "wellness" concept of living. The idea is to eat healthy, exercise frequently, supplement your diet with vitamins and natural nutrients and avoid excesses, whether it is food, alcohol, sweets, medications, or other harmful activities like smoking.

I am not a medical professional or nutritionist but there is a common sense approach to maintaining a healthy body. With over 60% of our adult population in the United States considered overweight and 30% classified as obese, it is obvious that many Americans are over-eating and under-exercising. There are a million diets and exercise regimens on the market, some are quite good, and others are totally without merit. Those diets that promise remarkable results with little effort on your part should be viewed with skepticism because they do not make sense. You have to experience some form of withdrawal or pain if you want to lose weight.

There is one weight control program that surpasses all others; it is the *Common Sense Diet*. The principle is simple and sensible: *you will gain weight when you take in more calories than you expend and you will lose weight when you expend more calories than you take in.* It is simple, but effective.

The idea is to find a happy balance for your diet and lifestyle that allows you to maintain a desired weight level. That does not imply that you need to be a calorie freak, far from it. I don't monitor my calorie in-take; I let the bathroom scale do it for me. When I gain a pound, I eat less and exercise more. If I lose a pound, I am more inclined to have a dish of ice cream as a reward.

If you eat plenty of fruits and vegetables and appropriate quantities of proteins, carbohydrates, grains, sweets, including moderate levels of alcohol, there is no need for a rigid diet plan. Just watch the dial on your bathroom scale and adjust your eating and exercise regimen accordingly.

There is theoretically no way that a person can gain ten or twenty or thirty pounds if you practice the Common Sense Diet. Remember that obesity occurs one ounce at a time. If you see the numbers on the scale going up, don't wait until they are 10 or 20 or 30 pounds overweight. The more pounds you are overweight, the harder it is to lose and the longer it takes. An extra pound or two gained can be removed in a few days with careful eating and exercise. The approach is to do something immediately to reverse the weight gain.

If you are experiencing serious weight problems as a result of a medical condition, or if you have other medical problems that might require professional guidance, you need to adjust your physical conditioning program to adhere to the professional advice of your doctor. Whatever your particular situation involves, you would be wise to do your best to care for your body. It is the only one you will ever have and today is the youngest you will ever be.

Finally, don't squander away the precious years of retirement in a diminished physical condition brought on by preventable health and body issues. You worked too hard during your career and have earned a right to enjoy your retirement to the fullest.

Even though I know that a Common Sense diet works, the whole idea of a "diet" is not the way to live a wholesome life. You should never be concerned about weight gain or loss if you maintain an active mind and body.

Three Keys to Maintaining a Healthy Lifestyle—the common sense approach to eating falls under the category of moderation. The other two components involve your mind and exercise.
1. Keep your mind active (reading, crossword puzzles, card games, study, etc.)
2. Make exercise a daily habit (especially with aerobic exercises like walking, running, bicycling, rowing, etc.)
3. Practice moderation in everything you do, especially eating and drinking (put the right things into your body in the right quantities, avoid excesses)

Need for Honesty

There are many other types of physical health issues that go unresolved simply because the person does not admit they have a problem or fail to ask for help. For instance, we had a very close family member who had a serious heart condition but he kept putting off the treatment. Sadly he suffered a massive heart attack and died a few days before he was scheduled for a checkup. If he had only accepted the fact that he had a problem and done something about it, chances are he might still be with us today.

Your must take a cold, hard look at your overall physical condition and make a list of things that you need to improve. Remember: if you don't do it now, you are jeopardizing your life and the future wellbeing of your partner and family.

Physical Improvement

After you complete the important physical requirements that you <u>need</u> to do, then you can consider all the other things that you might <u>want</u> to do to improve the physical appearance of your body. These are things that you don't need to do, you just would like to consider doing them.

There is nothing wrong with wanting to improve the physical appearance of your body, as long as you have first taken care of the physical health issues. If you want to improve your appearance, chances are you will feel better about yourself and that in turn will have favorable impact on your overall wellbeing. Whether it is a facelift or hair implant, if you really want to do it and it will make you feel better about yourself, then go for it.

It is important that you maintain the proper perspective about things that you do to make yourself feel and look younger. The reality is that each birthday is a reminder that you are getting older. You can't stop the clock but you can do lots of things to stay as "young" as possible both physically and mentally. We all know people who seem to defy their age by their ability to stay young looking and acting. It starts in the mind and then carries over into the body. If you think you are young, you will act young and you will do things that keep you feeling young.

If you are really interested in preserving your mind and body and staying young, you should read a book entitled *"Younger Next Year"* by Chris Crowley and Henry S. Lodge, M.D. The authors believe that as much as 70% of aging is optional. They postulate that many older people simply give in to the aging condition and stop trying to improve their mind and body. They developed seven rules to use in changing a person's approach to aging:

1. Exercise six days a week for the rest of your life.
2. Do serious aerobic exercise four days a week for the rest of your life.
3. Do serious strength training, with weights, two days a week for the rest of your life.
4. Spend less than you make.
5. Quit eating crap!
6. Care.
7. Connect and commit.

The steps above were quoted from their book. I urge you to read the book because it has the potential to help you enjoy your retirement years with a stronger and better functioning mind and body. But, you must first *want* to do it.

You also need to involve your doctor in your plan to ensure that you follow the appropriate treatment or medical guidelines. Your doctor should also establish the priorities and schedule for all of your planned improvements. It is important that you not bite off more than you can chew because you could run the risk of overwhelming yourself and lose your desire and momentum to improve.

The exciting thing about making the decision and commitment to improve your physical condition is that you will feel much better about yourself even before any of the problems are totally resolved. When you are physically fit, you simultaneously develop a very positive mental outlook on life.

Your goal is to make your body as strong as possible so that you can live longer and enjoy life more. If you fail to take care of your body, you run the risk of dying prematurely or developing a debilitating condition that could limit your activities.

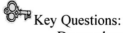 Key Questions:

- Do you have any physical issues that might impact your retirement plan?
- When will you schedule a routine physical exam with your doctor to identify any potential issues that need to be addressed?
- Have you and your doctor developed your key physical indicators (KPI)?
- What are your improvement targets for each key physical indicator?
- What specific actions will you take to improve your physical indicators?
- What is your plan for smoking, excess drinking, over the counter drug dependence?
- What is your plan for developing a healthy diet?
- Are there other physical issues that you don't need to do but that you want to do something about?
- When will you start?

Chapter 14

Personalized Retirement Plan:
Step #7—Mental Conditioning

"Why is it that our memory is good enough to retain the least triviality that happens to us, and yet not good enough to recollect how often we have told it to the same person?"
~Francois de La Rouchefoucauld

When I was younger I had a remarkable memory. I could see someone at a convention that I had not seen for years and come up with the name in a flash. I assumed that it was a capability that would endure throughout my entire life. Wrong. Sometime after age 50 or there about, all of us begin to lose a little of our memory function. We commonly refer to these lapses as "senior moments." The important thing in retirement is that we do whatever we can to prevent senior moments from becoming more frequent. The secret is *to do things that help to maintain your mental conditioning.*

The next important step is to address what you are doing now or plan to do in the future to maintain and enhance an active and healthy brain. Studies have shown that the brain will lose some of its memory and processing power if it is underutilized. Some of the loss is unavoidable as a result of natural aging and reduced blood flow to the brain, but there are definitely things you can do to preserve the capacity and functionality of your brain. It's much like physical exercise; the more you exercise the body, the healthier it is. Similarly, the more you use and exercise the brain, the healthier it will remain.

During your active career years, your brain got lots of stimulation as a result of your job and active lifestyle. Suddenly in retirement many people cut back dramatically on activities that formerly caused the brain to function at higher levels. The thought of not having to concentrate your mental powers might appear to be a blessing in the early days of retirement because one of the purposes of retirement is to rest and relax. If you don't continue to use your brain, you will lose some of your mental dexterity. Like the old saying goes, "Use it or lose it."

I'm not talking about innate intelligence or your I.Q. Whether you are a genius or something less, you need to do your best to exercise your brain and allow it to stay at the optimal performance level for as long as possible.

There are many proactive things you can to do to maintain an active brain and enhance your mental conditioning. Some of the alternatives include the following:

- **Lifelong Learning**—your retirement years present a tremendous opportunity to go back to "school" and restart your formal or informal education or learn some new trade, activity or hobby. You can select the school of your choice. Many communities offer various learning alternatives in local colleges or through public programs. For instance, in some states the public universities offer free tuition to any senior over age 70. In addition, most schools of higher education as well as churches and various organizations offer "adult education" or "continuing education" programs that are chocked full of interesting and expansive courses.

  One of my personal goals is to complete my studies to earn a Ph.D. Not only will it keep my mind active, it will be enormously rewarding to achieve something I have wanted to do my entire career.

  Another wonderful opportunity is the "distance learning" programs offered by countless schools and organizations. There are many fine educational institutions that offer complete courses that can be taken entirely online across the Internet. For instance, one site I am familiar with allows a person to become a certified real estate agent. Just get on your computer and look up "distance learning" or "lifelong learning" or "continuing education". You can also contact your community or state education boards for detailed information.

There are also many self-study programs you can subscribe to over the Internet or through the mail. Whatever the subject, there is a program that will help you learn more about something.

One of the advantages of going back to school as a retiree is that there is no pressure to get a "grade." You are there to learn and enjoy. The important thing is that any form of education or learning, whether formal or informal, will help you maintain a healthy and active mind.

- **Reading**—the act of reading is a tremendously rewarding mental exercise. It is a source of enjoyment, learning and mental expansion. It is through reading that we gain most of our knowledge. A person who reads is generally well versed on lots of topics and makes a wonderful conversationalist. A reader usually has an excellent vocabulary and is able to use language as an outlet for improving personal communication skills. And the best part is that reading is really inexpensive, particularly if you enroll in your local public library.

Incidentally, a day at the library is one of retirement's great treasures. Where formerly you might have used the library as a place to study or cram for an exam or find information for a last minute term paper, in retirement you can spend a day at the library and just enjoy looking around and learning what's available.

Every senior should have several books on their nightstand. Ideally there should be a book or two that you are reading for pure enjoyment. Another book should be on some contemporary subject or issue. The New York Times best seller list or your local newspaper is a wonderful guide to use in previewing books that you might want to read. The third type of book should be something on self-improvement. For instance, I like to read new books on business practice, especially marketing because that is my area of career interest. I find that they provide a wealth of information that helps to keep me current and open-minded.

On the other hand, you might want to focus your self-improvement reading on a totally new and different area. For instance, I have a friend who was an accountant during his career who focused his self-improvement goals on developing new language skills and is now fluent in French and Spanish, a great asset when traveling.

If your only source of reading is the newspaper and magazines, as informative as they might be, you need to be aware of the impact that technology is having on print media, especially newspapers. Most large newspaper companies are providing an online version of the paper to capture the market of younger, technically savvy people who grew up without newspapers.

In addition, the new electronic book readers (like Kindle) will revolutionize the way we buy and read books. It is now technically possible to download a vast number of books onto an electronic reader and create a personal library that you can take with you wherever you go. Imagine lying on a beach with one simple reading device that contains enough books to keep you reading for the rest of your life.

Reading is a great way to keep your mind healthy and alive.

- **Writing**—another wonderful outlet to improve your brain functioning is writing. You can try your hand at writing poems, short stories, novels of something as simple as compiling your own life history or writing informal letters to friends rather than emails or phone calls.

One of the sad realities of our contemporary culture is that we have inadvertently gotten away from passing along our personal and family history to our children and grandchildren. When I was a boy and prior to television and the other distractions of modern life, we regularly went to my grandparent's home for dinner on Sunday and after dinner we would gather on the floor around my grandfather and he would tell us stories about his youth and personal life experiences. He was passing down the experiences of his generation to us. As a result, he remains alive and vibrant in my memory.

My wife and I have found that our children and grandchildren really enjoy listening to stories about our early lives and personal stories about when they were babies and young children. Regrettably there will come a time when we will no longer be here to tell the stories, and then it will be too late to chronicle our history.

Suggestion: consider using your memory and writing skills to draft your own life history, sort of like writing your autobiography. If you are interested in family trees or genealogy or someone in your family has an interest in photography, you could literally compile a book complete with illustrations and pictures. Think about what a wonderful legacy it would be if you left your family with a complete life history from your generation. The process will help to keep your mind active and involved and become a treasure for your family long after you are gone.

- **Card and Table Games**—yes, there is an important place in your mental maintenance program for cards and table games, especially mentally taxing games like bridge or chess. The renewed interest in poker and gin are also outlets as long as they don't dominate your time or lead to excessive gambling. The key is to find an activity that causes you to challenge your brain.

One of the best mind-stretching activities is chess. Not all of us will be able to play at the master level, but a good game of chess with a friend or neighbor is an excellent way to exercise the brain.

- **Crossword Puzzles**—one of my favorite preoccupations is to work a good crossword puzzle. I think seniors may have a bit of an advantage at crosswords because there are many more things stored in our memory banks than in the experience base of younger people. There are things that seem to pop out of my memory when I'm working a crossword puzzle that is stored deep in my brain without being recalled for many years. The activity of racking your brain to recall a word is a tremendous way to keep your brain functioning. The Sudoku puzzles are also a tremendously fascinating and engaging mental activity, as are picture puzzles.

- **Music**—another terrific mental exercise is the playing of musical instruments. Many seniors have some music experience or instrument skills from their childhood that may have been ignored for many decades. Retirement is the time to dust off the old instruments and get back to playing music. For example, a good friend is a former bank executive and he has thrown himself into music as a major part-time retirement preoccupation. He not only dusted off the old trumpet, he practiced until he was good enough to try out for a local symphony orchestra. The challenge of reading music and learning how to play instruments is a wonderful way to keep the mind active. One of my other personal goals is to learn how to play the piano. We have a beautiful baby grand piano in our living room that represents another challenging opportunity for learning and personal growth.

- **Painting and Art**—one of the great artistic hobbies is painting. The beauty of painting and other artwork hobbies is that "beauty is in the eye of the beholder." The artist is able to transport themselves into a different dimension and allow their inner creativity to come to the surface. The challenges of learning how to paint or sculpt or create art provides a wonderful mental exercise. It can also become a lifelong pursuit. Importantly, it is something you can do the rest of your life since age is no barrier to creativity, remember Grandma Moses.

- **All Other Hobbies and Crafts**—there are so many things a retired person can do to provide both enjoyment and to reinvigorate their minds. I don't want to slight any activity but it is not possible to list all of them. The key is to find something that stimulates your brain and allows you to transport your mind into a different realm or dimension. When you become totally absorbed in your activity, your mind is working overtime to keep up with you. That's what you want and need in retirement. Another friend built a three-masted miniature sailing ship. He enjoyed the experience so much that he now has a whole houseful of miniature ships built totally inside a bottle.

Since we are all different with different tastes and skills and experiences, it is not possible to create a standard brain maintenance program for everyone, but rest assured that there is an activity or hobby or interest that you can use to maintain and stimulate your brain.

You don't ever want to lose any of your mental dexterity by failing to use your brain. If you engage in several of the above activities, it is likely that you will be able to maintain a strong and vibrant mind well beyond the normal aging cycle. If you are spending too much time on the couch in front of the TV, get up off your butt and exercise your body and your brain.

Key Questions:

- Do you plan to engage in any formal or informal learning program like adult education, continuous learning or distance learning?
- What specific activities will you engage in regularly and routinely to maintain and improve the condition of your brain? Reading? Writing? Painting? Music? Hobbies? Cards? Chess? Board games? Crossword puzzles? Sudoku? Part-time work? Volunteering?

Chapter 15

Personalized Retirement Plan:
Step #8—Lifestyle, Location and Leisure

"The ache of home lives in all of us, the safe place where we can go as we are and not be questioned."   ~Maya Angelou

One of the important issues to incorporate into your Personalized Retirement Plan is your feelings about how you want to live, or your lifestyle, where you want to live in your retirement years, and what you want to do with your time, both productive and leisure.

Lifestyle

First, let's define "lifestyle" to make sure everyone is on the same page. Lifestyle is a way of life or style of living that reflects the attitudes and values of a person or group. If someone were to ask you to describe your lifestyle, what would you say? It is a difficult question because most people are born into or gradually evolve into a lifestyle, not necessarily by conscious pre-thought. For instance, an urban dweller in a high rise apartment in New York City adapts to a different lifestyle than a farmer in Iowa or a suburban housewife in Seattle. Some people may have selected their lifestyle after evaluating various ways of living, but I suspect that most people are born into a certain lifestyle in their home town that becomes normal and natural. Therefore, an urban dweller would feel a little out of place on the farm in Iowa as would the farmer feel uncomfortable in the middle of Manhattan.

The process of developing a retirement plan provides you with the opportunity to evaluate your current lifestyle and determine if you want to make any changes. There are millions of transplanted retirees in the Sunbelt states who opted to change their lifestyle. Some of the transplants gave the new lifestyle a try and moved back to a more comfortable environment or comprised and relocated to an area that was a blend between the former and new lifestyles. For instance, the urban dwellers in Miami Beach may have been high rise tenants in Manhattan and like the idea of living high in the sky.

No one can impose a new lifestyle on you. If you are happy with the way you are living, then lifestyle may not be an issue. If you are adventurous and have an inner craving to try a new and different lifestyle, you have the power to make a decision and do it. The important thing is that lifestyle decisions do not have to be permanent. If you decide on relocating to a new area with a new way of living, and you don't like it, there is nothing wrong with reversing gears and returning to your former location, or trying another area. After all, it is your retirement and you can do whatever you want to do.

Lastly, lifestyle is partially determined by where a person lives, which is covered in the next section, but also is strongly influenced by a person's individual personality and attitudes. A cowboy from Wyoming can live quite well in New Orleans if he learns how to adjust and keeps an open mind. Some people have an easier time than others adapting and adjusting to new environments. The urban dweller and the farmer and the suburban housewife all have a unique personality and temperament that works in conjunction with their physical location to influence their lifestyle. The bottom line is that some people are simply more comfortable being in certain environments.

Location

There are two prevailing attitudes about where a person lives, before or after retirement. The first attitude embodies the *traditionalists*, who are born, live, work, and who will probably die in the same city, sometimes the same house. This group finds it difficult to imagine living anywhere else except in their home town and neighborhood.

There are exceptions but traditionalists are simply very comfortable with their life and the security that comes from family, friends, neighborhood, and the local support network.

Fact—even in the first decade of the 21st century, it is interesting to note that 87% of the people in the United States still live in the state of their birth (U.S. Census Data, 2000). So it is not unusual for many millions of seniors to prefer to work and live close to their original homestead.

I have three sisters who live in Ohio. Two sisters never lived more than a few miles from where they were born, as did their spouses. One sister relocated to California but moved back to Ohio after her spouse passed away to remarry and reconnect to the family. I was born in Ohio but for some reason I did not have the same instinctive feeling about my hometown. In fact, I was ready, willing, and anxious to relocate to the Sunbelt. Who knows what makes one person stay and the other leave?

But, it is important that both planning partners get on the same page about where they would like to live during retirement.

The second attitude about where a person lives involves the free-spirited *adventurers* who love change and who can hardly wait to relocate to a place of their retirement dreams. Although this group represents a minority of all retirees, they still account for millions of relocations, whether to Sunbelt states or to states that appeal to individual preferences, or even outside the United States. There is no one guideline to help you determine where you might want to live. You need to determine your preferences and then narrow down your options.

Best Places to Retire—one very helpful tool was created by *U.S. News & World Report* in their article, "Best Places to Retire" written by Tim Smart. The article provides a "search tool" you can use to evaluate your preferences by category: geographic region, weather, cost of living, recreational and cultural activities, social environment, health care, and crime. The tool allows you to determine the relative value you place on each category and then summarizes your values and suggests several places that you might consider for your retirement.

Go to http://www.usnews.com/directories/retirement.

One point to keep in mind is that the selection of a particular area is something that can be changed. If you move to an area and determine you are homesick or aren't satisfied with the lifestyle, there is nothing that prevents you from relocating again. For instance, the hurricanes and escalating housing costs in Florida changed the attitudes of many new retirees, as well as older established Floridians who packed up and headed north to Alabama, Georgia, and the Carolinas. In fact, the term "halfback" was coined to describe the seniors who moved halfway back from Florida.

Whether you are a traditionalist or an adventurer, there are several issues you should consider when planning where you might want to work and live in your retirement.

Compare New and Current Locations

It is easy to be influenced by travel brochures or articles or personal assessments of potential new locations, especially those in the Sunbelt states. The Chambers of Commerce do a great job of promoting their cities to attract retirees. It is very important that you conduct a very thorough research of your potential new location and compare all factors to your present location; including, cost of living, income taxes, city and country taxes, property taxes, utilities, mortgage rates, community maintenance or usage fees, heating and cooling costs, professional fees, initiation and dues for clubs, etc. Don't be swayed by those who might be more interested in making a sale than they are in providing full disclosure of all real or potential costs. In many instances, the total costs of the new location will be more than your present location.

You also need to compare other factors besides the financial implications. Some of the more important considerations include:

Weather—as the old saying goes, "Everyone talks about the weather but there is nothing we can do about it." Weather is what it is. It is important to make sure that you are comfortable with the actual weather patterns in your proposed new place of residence. You need to find out the average temperatures, rainfall, humidity, major weather events like tornadoes, hurricanes, earthquakes, droughts, floods, fires, etc. If you are moving from a colder climate to a much warmer climate, keep in mind that the summers will probably be much warmer than you have experienced. Some may like it, some may find it oppressive. For instance, southern Arizona has some beautiful weather in the spring, fall, and winter, but the temperatures routinely go over 100 degrees Fahrenheit in the summer months. Even with very low humidity, 100 plus temperatures take some getting used to.

The reality is that no place in the world has a perfect, ideal, year-round climate. You have to accept the good with the bad. Florida has great beaches and hurricanes; California has mild temperatures and wild fires and earthquakes; parts of Texas are wet, parts are very dry; South Carolina has Charleston and high humidity and bugs; Colorado has incredibly clear skies and rapidly changing weather. Each area has its strengths and weaknesses. Your job is to make sure you are compatible with the overall pattern of the weather.

Health Care—the issue of health care is an extremely important consideration in relocation. Retirees will require greater access to health care professionals and facilities. Based on your specific medical condition, you will need to determine what health care resources are important to you. Although you might want to retire to the wilderness, you must also be concerned about the location of the closest hospital and medical facilities. If you select an area that already has a sizable base of retirees, there will usually be adequate health care facilities.

Traffic—if you never lived in a major metropolitan area and you are considering moving to a larger city like Los Angeles, Phoenix, Miami, Houston, Orlando, Atlanta, etc., you are in for a monumental experience. Traffic does affect a person's lifestyle so make sure you consider where you might live and the local network of roads. Even if you plan to live in the suburbs, you need to realize that you still have to get into and through the city to experience all of the benefits of the new location. For instance, one of our relatives from a small town came to visit us in Atlanta and they were overwhelmed when they got stuck in rush hour traffic on an interstate that was eight lanes wide in one direction.

Local Culture and Traditions—if you are from the "north" and relocate the "south" or vice versa, you need to realize that your new location will have a unique culture that could be significantly different than your existing culture. Many regional areas have unique customs, language, food, drink, and local practices that are an important part of their heritage. You have to realize that there is a strong possibility that you might feel like a fish out of water until you become an established member of your new community. When we first relocated to the south, it was still fairly common to hear our neighbors refer to us as "Yankees", not in a derogatory sense, simply as identification. The beauty about the United States is our diversity and treasured differences between our ethnic cultures. One of the benefits of relocation is that there will probably be many more retirees in your same shoes who have moved from elsewhere around the country. In fact, most new retirees assimilate into their new community by getting involved in "newcomer" groups. When we moved to Georgia from Ohio, two of our next door neighbors also happened to be from Ohio so we had a lot in common.

Government and Politics—you will quickly recognize that all states, cities, and municipalities operate differently than where you come from. In addition, your new city and state might have a totally different political makeup. There really is a difference between the politics of the "blue" and "red "states. If politics is an important part of your life, make sure you select a new location that is compatible with your political views.

Cultural and Social Activities—if your present location has a significant numbers of museums, art galleries, the theatre, and other cultural benefits and you are relocating to an area that is quite distant from these amenities; you must place a value on the benefit and determine what you are willing to live without, or to a lesser degree of participation. If you want to be socially active, you need to live in a community or neighborhood that provides lots of social options. Many of the newer "over 55" communities cater specifically to the needs of seniors and retirees.

Lifestyle—various regions around the United States and the world have their own unique lifestyle. If is generally difficult for an urban dweller in a high-rise condo to quickly assimilate into a suburban or rural lifestyle when relocating to a one-floor duplex. The lifestyle in Texas is different than the lifestyle in Connecticut. It is important to evaluate the local lifestyle to ensure that it is compatible with your personal style and preferences, if not; the new location might tend to be a source of discontent.

Crime—crime is a national problem, but you have the opportunity to evaluate various cities by their crime rates, even to the neighborhood level. The crime rate also impacts lifestyle relative to safety and cost of living. Areas with higher crime rates also have higher insurance rates for homeowners' insurance, auto, and personal property riders.

Demographics—another important consideration is the overall demographics of your new potential location. If you are from a rural environment and relocating to a golf course condo community in southeast Florida, you will probably find that the bulk of your new neighbors are from urban areas. The differences might include educational backgrounds, incomes, professions, languages, ethnic traditions, etc. It is always a good idea to stick your toe in the water before jumping in head first.

Whatever you do, don't make a decision based on emotion. You can be comfortable and happy living anywhere in the world, including right in your existing home, because the most important consideration is not the location, but the value you place on your family, friends, and hometown heritage versus the potential benefits offered by the new location.

Cost of Living—the first point dealt with the overall cost comparisons between your current and potential new location. This point deals specifically with the cost of living in the new location. There are several websites that provide cost of living calculators that will allow you to compare costs by category for your current city versus your new city. Enter "cost of living calculators" in your browser.

(One good calculator is www.bankrate.com/brm/movecalc.asp)

The cost of living index includes key living costs like rent, food, transportation, utilities, taxes, services, entertainment, etc. The index provides an excellent comparison of the overall cost of living for the new location versus the current location. Be careful if the new location has a much higher projected cost of living because many retirees have a limited or fixed budget so the cost of living is important since very few costs ever decrease. Another important "cost" of living is the emotional cost that results from leaving family and friends, and the potential for additional trips to your former location to touch base and maintain your relationships. If you relocate from Maine to Florida, there will be substantial additional travel costs, both for you and your family. You need to consider additional travel expense for family events, weddings, funerals and reunions.

Family, Friends, Church and Community—the cold reality of a relocation is that you will separate yourself from your family, friends, church, and community. Many millions of people have done it so it is not an insurmountable task; it is just something that you must evaluate based on your own set of circumstances. If you are very close-knit family, it will be more difficult to cut the family umbilical. Most people who were transferred during their careers are better prepared to cope with relocation because they understand the pain and anguish of not being immediately available to your extended family. If you have never lived in another house or city during your pre-retirement years, you need to make sure you really want to relocate. One option might be to spend a month or more in the proposed new location just to get a feel for what it is like. A person never really understands how difficult it is to relocate until they actually do it. It is particularly difficult on the mother in the family who has a unique bond with her children. Many parents have expressed how depressed they became after relocation because they felt they had abandoned their children, or felt guilty that they were not available to continue nurturing them.

Support Network—a very important consideration is to recognize the potential significance of your personal support network, namely those close to you who will watch over and take care of you when you have an illness or an extended physical problem. In your present location you might be able to rely upon children, grandchildren, brothers or sisters, close relatives, or friends to lend a hand, short or long range. If you relocate to a new location that is distant from your existing support network, who will you be able to depend on for help? In the event that one partner passes away, what is the plan for your support network? The fact is that everyone ages and most people will eventually require some degree of assistance. Be sure to plan wisely on determining your support network.

Professional Relationships—one of the more difficult challenges facing seniors who relocate is establishing new relationships with doctors, dentists, attorneys, accountants and all the other professionals who have been providing services for several decades. In addition, there will be a need to transfer all the medical and personal records. It is a difficult task to re-establish relationships with new professionals when your current team has provided you with advice and counsel and who know you and your family intimately.

Starting Over—the relocation process is much like starting all over in a marriage or relationship. Everything is new or different. It is both frustrating and rewarding. It is frustrating because nobody knows you and you don't know anybody. Where previously all you had to do was make a phone call and things were taken care of. Now you have to figure out who you are going to call, then determine if they are capable and compatible, and then repeat your needs over and over. It is also rewarding because in your new location you have the opportunity to select your new friends and the people who want to get involved with. If you will be retiring with children or parents or dependents, you must keep in mind that they too will be emotionally involved in the assimilation process. You should expect that the transition will not be painless or easy.

Compatibility—the best advice for anyone planning to relocate is to do your homework and make sure that you really want to give up an important part of your past for a potentially more rewarding new experience. You should feel comfortable that you are jumping into something that is actually compatible with your new planned lifestyle. If you are a stay-at-home person, don't expect that you will suddenly change to a country-club activist, in spite of the ads you might see on TV for some retirement communities. Most people have the same wants, needs, and personalities in retirement that they had during their career. As a wise philosopher once said, "You are what you are because you are." It is unlikely that you will change very much, regardless of where you live.

Leisure

The other important component of your lifestyle is what you do in your productive and leisure time. Some people go into retirement with the notion that their days will be spent solely on leisure activities. Many avid golfers or tennis players relocated to a golf/tennis community so they could play their favorite sport almost non-stop. For some, it remains a wonderful way of life; others quickly tire of the leisure activities and long for a return to a more normal existence. It is simply that some people are not cut out to spend all of their time on leisure activities.

The key is balance, or a balanced lifestyle that combines productive activity, family, friends, spiritual, community and leisure activities. It is also true that one man's feast is another man's poison. This phenomenon can be seen up close and personal in outlet malls around the country where the shopper in the family is enthusiastically shopping every single store in search of the latest and greatest values. For the shopper this is an ultimate leisure time activity, but for the spouse it may be sheer torture so they find the closest snack bar or rest area and promptly take a nap.

Leisure is personal and varied. A golfer can also be a stamp collector or music hound. A chess player or bridge expert can also be addicted to baseball or football. An avid runner can also be a master chef. Once again the issue of balance is important; a person tires of doing the same old, same old every day, but there is nothing wrong with mixing leisure time activities throughout the day or week to provide a higher level of personal satisfaction.

The truly well-rounded retiree is one who blends leisure activities with other rewarding activities in their work, church or community. The leisure activities provide personal satisfaction; the volunteer activities provide the opportunity to strive for a higher level of satisfaction and personal fulfillment.

Key Questions:

- How would you describe your current lifestyle?
- What do you like about your lifestyle?
- What don't you like? Your partner?
- Are you content to continue your current lifestyle in retirement? Any lifestyle changes? Why?
- Where do you want to live in retirement? Why?
- Where will you live when you might need assistance?
- What leisure activities do you want to pursue? To what extent? Your partner?
- How much of your time do you want to devote to leisure? How much to work? Volunteering? Personal development?
- What is your ideal balance between all activities? Your partner?
- Have you compared all of the characteristics of a new potential location? Weather? Traffic? Healthcare? Cultural and social activities? Crime? Cost of Living? Impact of family, friends, church and community? Support network? Professional relationships? Compatibility?

Chapter 16

Personalized Retirement Plan:
Step #9—Exit Strategy

"Of all the wonders that I yet have heard, it seems to me most strange that men should fear; seeing that death, a necessary end, will come when it will come."   *~William Shakespeare*

One of the most important steps in creating your PRP is to anticipate and plan for your death. You have a responsibility and obligation to review and complete your legal and personal requirements, specifically your will, the living will provision, your funeral plans, and your personal instructions for your estate and family. I borrowed the term "exit strategy" from the venture capitalists who always include a plan to exit an investment when certain benchmarks are reached. It is a good term to use for planning and preparing for your eventual exit from this world.

Most people are not comfortable talking about death. Once you accept the reality and put your passing in the category of another thing you need to discuss and plan for, then you can move forward and fulfill your obligation to your partner and family. Below are some suggestions to help you discuss and complete this step in the preparation of your PRP.

There are two areas of planning that you absolutely must address when developing your exit strategy: your *legal requirements* and your *personal preferences*.

Important Guideline from the Author
I am not an attorney. I cannot give advice or counsel on your particular needs. It is your responsibility to find a competent attorney and estate planner. The comments below are generalized guidelines that are presented only for informational purposes and may not be applicable to your particular circumstances or place of residence.

Legal Requirements

From a legal perspective, you need to prepare an "estate plan" that would include your last will and testament, advance health directives, various powers of attorney, and the designation of executors and administrators. You need an estate plan whether you are a multi-millionaire or pension-check-to-pension-check retiree. You do not want to die without a will or your various directives. It won't matter to you when your ashes are spread to the wind, but it will certainly complicate life for your partner and family.

Although some people have a difficult time dealing with the hereafter issues, it is a necessity and the wise thing to do to protect your hard-earned assets and to ensure peace within your family. The failure to prepare an estate plan could result in the payment of excess taxes and fees. If you have not yet done so, don't wait another day before you call an attorney and arrange for a meeting to discuss the legal implications of your eventual passing, or check out various websites on the Internet for will-making software and requirements.

One source is LegalZoom at http://www.legalzoom.com/wills-estate-planning/wills-estate-planning.html

❑ **Estate Planning**—this is the process of planning what you want to happen to your assets. There are four important components of your estate plan: **last will and testament, advance health directives, powers of attorney**, and the designation of the **executor and administrators** of our estate.

It is absolutely vital that you use an attorney and a financial advisor when preparing your estate plan. The average lay person is not capable of understanding all of the laws, rules and regulations that come into play after you die. If you do not use a trained professional, you run the risk of jeopardizing a sizable portion of your estate. Your attorney and financial advisor work with you to minimize potential taxes and fees and determine what you want to happen with your home, property, investments, business, life insurance, employee benefits (such as a pension plan), and other tangible assets. It is important that you create your estate plan while you are still physically and mentally capable of making the decisions.

On the personal side, an estate plan includes directions to your spouse, partner or family to carry out your personal wishes regarding health care matters, including advance directives, living will, and various powers of attorney.

Lastly, the estate plan provides the opportunity to designate your executor, trustee, and legal guardians for your estate.

❑ **Last Will and Testament**—the last will and testament represents the most recent, existing, legitimate will before you die, nullifying all previous wills and testaments. The last will and testament provides you with the right to specify how you want your property and possessions to be allocated or disposed of. The phrase implies the legal existence of the document on the grounds that there is no other will or testament executed after that date to supersede it. The terms "will and testament" means basically the same thing. The last will and testament is preferably created with the assistance of an estate planning attorney.

There are numerous sad stories about families who have been torn apart by the failure of the patriarch or matriarch to create and communicate a last will and testament. Unfortunately, the disposition of assets in a will can lead to disagreements and disputes within a family, all of which can be avoided by clearly spelling out your wishes and then communicating your wishes to your family before you die.

❏ **Advance Directives**--advance directives are written instructions regarding your end-of-life medical care preferences. You should consult with your attorney for a more personal discussion of your particular needs relative to advance directives. The intent is to provide the opportunity to express your feelings and instructions to your spouse and family members about how you would like to have decisions made about your health care when you are not physically or mentally capable. There are three types of advance directives you should consider adding to your estate plan; living will, medical or healthcare power of attorney, and a do-not-resuscitate order.

Living Will—this is a written, legal document that spells out the types of medical treatments and life-sustaining measures you do or don't want, such as mechanical breathing, tube feeding, and resuscitation. A living will allows you to make decisions about your body that could be extremely difficult or painful if you leave the decision to your spouse or children.

A Life or Death Decision

I know from personal experience the burden and pressure that is put on a family to do the right thing at a time when you are not emotionally capable of making a life or death decision. My mother suffered a severe stroke following a major surgery. The doctors gave her practically no chance to survive and if she did survive, she would have extremely limited mental capability. She was on life support equipment and we had to make a decision for our mother because she did not have a living will. After much prayer and reflection, we asked that she be removed from life support equipment. We expected that she would die quickly, but in some miraculous manner she survived and lived another 15 years, although she never regained her full mental or physical capacity. This is not a decision you want to leave for your spouse and children.

In some states, the living will may be known by a different name, such as health care declaration or health care directive.

Medical or Healthcare Power of Attorney (POA)—this is also called a *durable power of attorney for health care* or a *health care agent or proxy*. The medical POA is a legal document that designates an individual that will make medical decisions in your behalf in the event you're unable to do so. The medical POA allows your designated agent to interpret your wishes when unexpected developments aren't specifically addressed by your living will.

The "medical POA" document is different from the standard power of attorney form that authorizes a designated person to make legal or financial decisions for you. If you don't appoint a medical POA, the decisions about your care will usually default to your spouse or designated partner. If you aren't legally married, decisions normally are made by your adult children or your parents.

A medical power of attorney allows you to designate a person who will have the authority to make health care decisions on your behalf if you are unconscious, mentally incompetent, or otherwise unable to make such decisions. In many states you can also express your wishes regarding whether you wish to receive "life-sustaining procedures" if you become permanently comatose or terminally ill. A medical power of attorney is used in conjunction with a living will. In the living will you specify your end-of-life health care preferences. If your condition is covered by the living will, you made the decision in advance. If your condition is not specifically covered in the provisions of your living will, then a medical POA allows a designated third party to make decisions in your behalf.

Do not resuscitate order (DNR)—there is another option that some people use to ensure that there is no misunderstanding about their end-of-life preferences. The do-not-resuscitate order (DNR) is a request to not have cardiopulmonary resuscitation (CPR) if your heart stops or if you stop breathing when the likelihood of survival is remote or when you may live in a vegetative state. A DNR order can be put in your medical chart by your doctor.

Living wills and medical powers of attorney have limitations. For instance, you can't possibly plan ahead for every situation, so what you include in your living will might not apply in certain instances. Your medical POA isn't given a set of instructions on what to do in every situation, so you have to trust that this person will make decisions based on what they perceive to be your intent.

The ideal approach to ensuring that your living will and directives are understood is to talk them over with your spouse and family. Tell them why you arrived at a particular course of action. This provides your loved ones with a greater insight into what you would desire in specific medical situations.

It would be tragic if something happened to you or your partner and you were not able to express your wishes about what you want done to preserve or end your life in an accident or critical illness. It is vital that you prepare a living will to provide your partner and family with the necessary legal requirement to support your decision.

Clark Howard, a preeminent consumer advocate, has helped millions of people deal with financial and personal challenges (check out his website www.clarkhoward.com). Clark said, "People should write exactly what they would like to happen in what's called an advance directive. People should also appoint a messenger who will be the steward of that information and will deliver it to the appropriate parties if something happens." It's important to establish your wishes ahead of time.

Additional Resources for Living Wills and Directives

- www.partnershipforcaring.org (provides specific advance directive forms for each state)
- www.agingwithdignity.org (offers details about the Five Wishes document)
- www.healthdirectives.org (charges a fee to scan directive documents and make wallet-sized cards specifying how medical providers can retrieve the documents from the website)
- www.uslivingwillregistry.com (offers directive services for member hospitals).

Sometimes we tend to think that tragedies happen only to other people, but remember that all of the people who are currently being treated in the emergency rooms in hospitals across the country thought the same thing. There is no reason to take a chance on your life. It makes sense for you to incorporate a living will component into your will. Your attorney will have several drafts of living will statements for you to review. In the absence of a living will, you could jeopardize your future well-being and that of your partner and family.

For example, a recent case in Florida illustrates the point. A young woman in her mid-20s suffered a severe stroke triggered by an eating disorder. The stroke permanently damaged her brain and left her in a state of perpetual coma. She did not have a living will and the decision about preserving her life evolved over several years into a family dispute that spilled over into the community and nation. She was kept alive in a vegetative state by a feeding tube while the husband, parents, and legal experts argued the case all the way up to the Supreme Court. Unfortunately no one could ask the patient her opinion. The controversy, pain, and expense could have been avoided if there was a living will.

This tragic case also illustrates the point that living wills are not just for seniors and retirees. When it comes to accidents and illness, fate does not differentiate between ages. Every adult, married or single, should have a living will.

Hopefully it will not take a similar event in your family to impress upon you the importance of a living will. If you personally do not express your wishes, while you are able to, the decision will be left to your spouse, partner or family, the doctors or hospital in the event of an accident or serious illness. Don't place this burden on them without your input.

There are other key appointments that you should consider incorporating into your will or advance directives. I would like to reiterate that I am not an attorney. These descriptions were provided from information located on the Internet at www.legal-definitions.com Your best source for legal advice and counsel is your personal attorney.

Power of Attorney (POA)—A power of attorney is a legal instrument used to delegate legal authority to another person. The person who signs or executes a POA is called the *principal.* The person who is designated at the legal authority is called an *agent or attorney-in-fact.* POA gives legal authority to your agent to make decisions for you concerning property, financial, and other legal requirements.

A principal can give an agent broad legal authority, or very limited authority. The POA is frequently used when a principal is temporarily ill or disabled or involving legal transactions where the principal cannot be present to sign necessary legal documents.

A "Nondurable" Power of Attorney is often used for a specific transaction, like the closing on the sale of residence, or the handling of the principal's financial affairs while the principal is traveling outside of the country.

A "Durable" Power of Attorney enables the agent to act for the principal even after the principal is not mentally competent or physically able to make decisions. The "Durable" POA may be used immediately, and is effective until it is revoked by the principal, or until the principal's death.

Executor—an executor is the person appointed in your will to administer your estate. Unless there is a valid objection, the judge will appoint the person named in the will to be executor. The executor must ensure that the desires of the deceased that are expressed in the will are carried out. Practical responsibilities include gathering up and protecting the assets of the estate, obtaining information in regard to all beneficiaries named in the will and any other potential heirs, collecting and arranging for payment of debts of the estate, approving or disapproving creditor's claims, making sure estate taxes are calculated, forms filed and tax payments made, and in all ways assisting the attorney for the estate.

Administrator—an individual appointed by a probate court to handle the estate of a person who died intestate (without a legal will). The administrator has the same duties as an executor.

Trustee—an individual or organization that will hold or manage or invest the assets of the estate. The trustee is legally obliged to make all trust-related decisions with the trustee's interests in mind, and may be liable for damages in the event of not doing so. Trustees may be entitled to a payment for their services, if specified in the trust deed.

Guardian—a person legally entrusted with the care of, and managing the property and rights of, another person, usually a minor.

Personal Preferences

The other component of the estate plan deals with the personal things that you want to specify before you go to the great beyond. In the prior sections, the intent of the legal instruments is to provide guidance and direction for your family and the courts. You have an obligation to determine how you want your property, belongings, and financial resources to be distributed in compliance with all legal and tax issues. The intent of the personal directions is to provide your spouse and family with guidelines about non-legal issues, specifically, your funeral plans and personal preferences.

Exit Discussion--before you delve into the details, you should start this part of your planning with an open and frank discussion with your spouse, partner, and family about death. Although some people are uncomfortable talking about death, there is no way to avoid the reality that we will all die some day. If you are open to discussing death, then you can move forward and answer the questions below. If you are reluctant to talk about it, you need to overcome your anxiety and build up your inner strength to face the reality as best you can.

The intent of the exit discussion is to provide you with the opportunity to talk about and determine how you want things to be handled at your funeral and beyond. My wife and I have given it a lot of thought and found that it was not as difficult as we had imagined. We discussed and agreed on several basic issues and incorporated them into our wills as a guideline for our children. Below in an excerpt from a typical will that will provide you with insights into the kind of things you need to discuss.

Personal Preferences

"The detailed instructions for our preferences are contained in an attachment to our wills. The surviving partner will honor the wishes of the other unless both partners decease together. The family will honor the wishes of both parents if they decease together. It is our desire that our bodies be given to medical research (include name of medical institution). When the research is completed, the bodies will be cremated and returned to the family for burial. At the time of our decease, we do not want a viewing or expensive funeral. We want a simple ceremony conducted as quickly as practical. Since our body will not be present, the family can select a favorite picture that can be placed in a prominent position at the front of church. We have selected the songs, hymns, and vocalist. We would like to have our children, grandchildren, family, and friends participate in a "celebration of life." After the service we want to have a traditional Irish wake with a large montage of pictures and remembrances from our lives that can serve as a reminder of our wonderful life experience. We desire that everyone celebrate our lives, not mourn our death. The cremated ashes are to be placed in an urn by the surviving partner, or children, who will mingle the ashes of both partners into one urn and bury them in a predetermined place. The detailed instructions, including our obituaries, are specified in our last will and testament."

Some might think that this level of planning is excessive, but you have to remember that the planning for your funeral is much like the planning you went through for your marriage. Most people put a lot of planning into their wedding because it is one of the most important days of your lives. The day of your death is the culmination of your life so why not put a similar amount of planning into your funeral?

You will find that it is not as difficult as you might think, once you get over the reality that some day it will all come to pass, not whether but when.

Funeral arrangements—you have the opportunity to decide if you want a traditional funeral home program including casket, wardrobe, flowers, viewing, headstone, burial vault, etc. You need to determine the type and cost of the casket and the related services. It is extremely important that you resolve these issues before you die because it is possible that your partner might make decisions based on emotion rather than your preferences.

Rest assured, the deceased doesn't care if they are interred in a wooden box, a gold plated casket or a ceramic urn. You need to make decisions rationally, not emotionally.

The Green Burial Movement
There is a new trend in funerals and burials that is referred to as the "green burial movement." A "green" burial is a natural burial without embalming in which the body or cremated remains are buried very simply in a plain wooden casket or ceramic urn, or even a simple shroud without a casket. The concept relates to the quotation from the book of Genesis, "Dust thou art and unto dust shalt thou return." The intent is to allow burial to be more eco-friendly and provide an option to reduce the cost of a contemporary funeral. One example is Honey Creek Woodlands in Conyers, GA that offers spaces for simple, traditional, natural burial as well as spaces for cremated remains. For more information on Honey Creek Woodlands and the Green Burial Movement, go to www.honeycreekwoodlands.com or directly to the Green Burial Council at
http://naturalburial.coop/USA/green-burial-council/

You have the opportunity to determine all of the details of your funeral whether it is conducted in the funeral home, a church or synagogue or at the gravesite. You can specify all of the details or exercise your option for a no frills funeral. You have the opportunity to create the type of service that is compatible with the kind of person you are and what you consider to be best for your spouse and family.

Funerals come in all shapes and sizes. You can spend as much as you want or as little as need be, it's your call. One of the big expense factors is whether you want to be buried or cremated. Traditional body burials with full funeral home services are the most expensive. The trend is toward more cremations. According to the Cremation Society of America, in the U.S. in 1979, only 10% of deaths were cremated. It is expected to rise to over 55% by

2025. The western and mountain states are currently ahead of the trend with over 60% of deaths resulting in cremation. The lowest rate of cremation is in the southern states with cremation around 10%. Some countries, notably Japan, are already at 98%.

If there is one guideline to follow it is simply to do it your way, but make sure you let your spouse and family know your desires so they don't spend a lot of money on things that won't really matter once you are in the ground.

A funeral is perhaps the most sober thing any of us can participate in. It is a sad occasion to have a loved one or friend die, especially when it is sudden and unexpected. In recent years there has been another movement that focuses on a "celebration of life" rather than the agony of death. The grief and remorse are natural but the reality is that the deceased is truly in a better place. If he or she had lived a good life, there is every reason to celebrate the occasion and join with family and friends to be thankful for being a part of a wonderful life experience.

My Brother-in-Law's Funeral

When my brother-in-law passed away a few years ago he had a beautiful, but simple service. The cremation urn sat on a table in the sanctuary of the church, draped in purple, with a portrait placed next to the urn. Four friends and relatives gave eulogies that were upbeat and positive. Each eulogist gave a personal tribute in which they remembered the fun things in their shared experiences. Each eulogy touched on the personal qualities of the deceased in the form of a personal tribute. The hymns were personal favorites. It was a beautiful service. After the service, everyone was invited to their home for a celebration of life. The daughters spent hours creating a beautiful and creative montage of pictures of their father and the family, starting as a kid and all the way through weeks prior to his death. It provided everyone with the opportunity to see what a wonderful and full life he had experienced. It also affirmed in our minds that a little planning in advance results in the type of service that fits the life and style of the deceased.

Post-funeral activity—some people may opt to get the whole thing over with as soon as possible. Many families will schedule a luncheon or dinner or party after the funeral to provide a time for bonding and reinforcing the love and support that is necessary when you lose a loved one. Whatever is your preference, you have the right to plan for your post-funeral activity.

Our family tradition after a funeral is to have a social affair similar to an Irish wake. The family and friends get together to toast and remember the deceased. It is a time of joy and thanksgiving rather than a time of sorrow and regret. The process is actually the beginning of the healing process because there is an awareness of finality and acceptance. It also helps the grieving partner and family members to put their loved one's life into perspective. The sadness of the funeral is balanced by the joy and companionship of the wake.

Obituary—the writing of one's obituary provides the opportunity to condense an entire life experience into a few paragraphs. It is always much easier to write a long letter than a short note.

Brevity is an Art

I recall a story told about Sir Winston Churchill after World War II. Sir Winston was living in retirement and was asked by a prominent local women's club to give a keynote speech for their annual meeting. Sir Winston advised that he would be delighted to give the speech and asked how long of a presentation they desired. When the chairperson replied that that he would be allotted only 15 minutes on their busy program, Sir Winston responded with a simple note that said, "Dear Madam, I must regretfully decline your kind offer to address your group, but I simply do not have the time to prepare for a 15 minute speech."

It would have been quite easy for Sir Winston to ramble on extemporaneously about his lifetime experiences for hours and hours, but he realized that it would take quite a lot of time to condense his thoughts into a short speech.

Your obituary presents a similar challenge. How do you condense an entire lifetime experience into a few paragraphs or a single page? It forces you to think about what is really important in your life and what is trivial and insignificant.

Perhaps the shortest and most succinct obituary I ever read stated, "I was born. I died. In between, I lived." Underneath a sense of humor was a rather profound understanding of life. There is a beginning, there is an end, and there is life in between. The beginning and ending are easy to write about, but it's the "in between" stuff that represents the challenge.

Earlier I touched on two issues that should help in gathering your thoughts about what is really important in your life. The first was the identification of your strengths, or those things that you are really good at. The second was the extension of your strengths into your core competency or that one thing that represents your greatest capability.

If you are able to identify your greatest strength and core competency, it can serve as the foundation for capturing your "in between" accomplishments.

Most obituaries are long, detailed summaries of relatives' names, schools attended, jobs and titles, awards and recognitions, activities, etc. In fact, some of the obituaries in newspapers appear to be contests to see who has the longest obituary. However, the most important statistic in all of our lives is whether we have treated everybody in a way that we ourselves would like to be treated. If you have led a giving life, you are a good person and you deserve your heavenly reward, regardless of how many initials you have after your name or the length of your obituary. Wouldn't a brief synopsis of the person be better?

Your obituary should be simple, brief and to the point. There is no need to chronicle every event or accomplishment in your life, just hit the highlights, including:

- Birth date and location
- Deceased date, location and cause (optional)
- Parents names, whether living or deceased
- Names of spouse, children, grandchildren, great grandchildren and locations
- Occupation and career highlights
- Funeral arrangements, date and time
- Preferences for remembrances

You can write longer obituaries but the reality is that nobody reads them anyway. The writing of your obituary allows you to focus on what is really important in your life.

Headstone Inscription—if you choose to have a traditional burial with a grave and headstone, you need to determine where you want to be buried and what you want to have engraved on your headstone. Don't take anything for granted.

The determination of where you will be buried is tied to family tradition and heritage in many families. If you go to any cemetery you will find many examples of families who have several generations clustered together in one larger plot. If you or your partner's have this tradition in your family, you need to determine if you will continue the tradition or break away.

There are many examples where family members have moved to faraway places while their family burial plot is still back where they were born. Some traditional families have members who will live and die within a few miles of where they were born. It is difficult for them to think that a son or daughter wouldn't automatically opt to be buried in their original homestead. If you are from a family like this, it is better to discuss it now so there are no misunderstandings.

Remember: it is your life, your body, and your funeral. You need to decide where you want to be buried or where you ashes will be placed.

The next issue is the engraving on your headstone, if you decide to have one. Most inscriptions are very simple, just the name and birth and death dates, maybe with a simple tag line indicating mother or father or son or daughter. On the other hand, there are some elaborate and monumental headstones in the cemeteries of the world.

Some people put strange things on their headstones. In fact, there is a pictorial book about unusual headstones. Two of my favorite inscriptions are: "I told you I was sick!" The other inscription was by the spouse of a philanderer who engraved, "At last I know where he is sleeping tonight."

Another consideration about cemeteries and headstones is that they add some additional expense to a funeral and perhaps an additional expense into the future for maintenance.

On the Loss of a Partner—once the grieving over the loss of a partner has been accepted, the next step is to contemplate life without that partner. It is an important part of your PRP because it provides you with the time to discuss your feelings about what you want the other partner to consider after you decease.

For instance, the biggest question is whether or not the surviving partner should remarry? Although there is never one best answer, it is something that you need to express an opinion about.

If one partner has been very dependent on the other, it will be very difficult to live without them, or without someone else that they can depend on. There are lots of examples of partners, men in particular, who remarry very quickly after a long term partner deceases. The principal reason is that some people simply cannot live very well without another person in their everyday lives, whether it is for the practical issues of cooking and housekeeping, or physical companionship, or both.

If you are a male spouse and your wife buys all your clothes, prepares all the meals, does all the shopping, runs the house, pays the bills, and packs for your trips, there is a significant chance that you will have a very difficult time living alone.

One of the other important issues is the integration of the families of both partners after a partner remarries. Although most children are happy to see their mothers or fathers remarry, there are some situations where the children become very upset about having "new" parents and families in their lives. Suddenly there are "his", "hers" and perhaps "our" children involved.

If you are a surviving spouse and are considering another marriage, it is important to keep in mind that you should do what makes you happy. Your deceased spouse, if he or she could talk, would encourage you to follow your heart. You can seek the advice and counsel of your children and other family members but you have to decide what is in your best interest. It is important that both spouses, prior to any death, should be willing to express an opinion about remarriage. Who better to ask than the person who shared your life for a very long time?

One situation I am aware of involved a remarriage when a man's spouse deceased. After almost 15 years of marriage to the new spouse, he became seriously ill and passed away. The children from his first marriage contested his will in which he left his second wife the bulk of his estate. If you know or suspect that there might be this kind of issue in your family, it is best to address it before you remarry or before you decease by stating your intentions in your will. It is your right and obligation to tell your family what you want to happen to your resources.

In another personal example, my mother remarried about 10 years after my father died and the man she married had three younger children. I was in college and suddenly I had stepbrothers and sisters who were in their early elementary school years. We were not a very compatible group, another key issue to consider.

Another friend lost a wife to cancer and was married within four months and his children were very supportive. There is no guideline for how long a couple should date before they marry whether it is the first or second time or more. Likewise there are no guidelines on whether or when someone might remarry. The only admonition is to discuss the issues in advance to avoid as many problems as possible within the family.

Remember: the intent of your retirement years is to enjoy life, not to get embroiled in family problems. The more you can spell out before you go to the Great Beyond, the better.

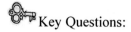 Key Questions:

Estate Planning Issues:
- Do you and your partner have an up-to-date last will and testament?

- Do you have an attorney who understands your will and requirements? Will your attorney be available during our retirement years?
- Have you prepared Advanced Directives (living will, medical power of attorney, and do-not-resuscitate orders) that spell out what you want done in the event you are incapacitated?
- Do you have a power of attorney document that specifies who is legally allowed to make decisions in your behalf?
- Have you determined, or updated, your executor, administrator and trustee for handling the details your last will and testament?

Personal Requirements:
- Have you had an "exit discussion" with your spouse, partner and family members to advise them of your wishes after you are deceased?
- Have you discussed and written down your funeral wishes? Where? Formal, informal, private, public? Who officiates? Pall bearers? Eulogists? Hymns? Prayers? Post-funeral reception and arrangements?
- Have you written or provided your family with the highlights of your obituary?
- Have you specified your burial wishes? Where? Cremation? Burial?
- Have you determined if you want a headstone? The inscription?

Chapter 17

Personalized Retirement Plan:
Step #10—Integrate Financial Planning

"If money is your hope for independence you will never have it. The only real security that a man will have in this world is a reserve of knowledge, experience, and ability."   ~Henry Ford

This is not a financial planning book. The central theme has been that *financial planning* has tended to dominate *retirement planning*. There is a perceived mental link between the two terms and they tend to be used interchangeably. But, in fact, financial planning is a subset or component of retirement planning. The purpose of this book has been to provide you with the tools to use in preparing a whole and complete retirement plan, including the financial component.

There are a great many seniors who are caught in an ironic "Catch 22". If you started to work with a financial planner several decades ago and implemented a good savings and investment plan, you might have gotten the impression that your retirement concerns were well taken care of. The catch is that your financial plan is only one component of a comprehensive retirement plan. You may have enough money to retire comfortably but the issue is simply, "What now?" What is your game plan for all the other things that you want or need to do in retirement?

I have enormous respect for financial planners, but you must keep in mind that their focus is money, not all of the issues that make up your retirement experience. The problem is that too many seniors are led to believe that if you get your financial house in order, everything else will fall into place. Take it from an experienced retiree that is not the case. In addition to your financial plan, you need to consider a great many other issues.

I made the decision to put "integrating financial planning" as the 10th step in developing your retirement plan. I don't imply that you should wait until you retire to begin your financial planning; you need to begin your savings and investment program early in your career. But, I do suggest that *retirement planning* is the number one priority. It provides the macro view of retirement. It establishes many of the boundaries for how you can use your financial resources to maximize your retirement experience. It serves as the balance point between what you might want to do with what you will be able to afford. Once you have completed the first nine steps in your Personalized Retirement Plan, you are then prepared to integrate your financial plan into your overall retirement plan.

Some people might differ with my point of view that financial planning is one of the concluding steps in creating your PRP. I understand and appreciate that point of view. However, there is a difference between when you "start" the financial planning process and when you integrate your financial plan into your retirement plan.

There are two important points to keep in mind. First, it is absolutely vital that you have a financial plan. Second, you should start the financial planning process as early as possible in your career. Ideally, the financial planning should begin in the first few years of a person's career because it takes a lifetime of savings and investment to create a retirement nest egg that will be sufficient for an individual to live comfortably in retirement. Those who delayed the process or never committed to the need to build a retirement savings program will be at a distinct disadvantage when they begin their retirement, if they are able to retire at all.

Key Point: Develop a relationship with a qualified financial advisor early in your career and make a commitment to save and invest conservatively to ensure that your financial nest egg is adequate to support your retirement lifestyle.

The paradox of retirement planning is that you can find an untold number of financial advisors and financial planning models and computer programs to help you create a financial plan, but you will find practically nothing that addresses the need for a master retirement plan. The fact is that financial planning is but one part of a comprehensive retirement plan. You need it but the amount of money you have in retirement is relevant to what you intend to do in your retirement.

The Rest of the Story...

Paul Harvey coined the phrase, "And now, the rest of the story..." There is another really important reason why the retirement planning process should take priority over financial planning. You will find that the most important things in retirement are centered on personal relationships, especially the relationship with your spouse or partner. Money is important, but money cannot buy or improve a relationship. Relationships are built and improved by developing a personal understanding and empathy for the other person's wants and needs. It is when you give of yourself to someone that you receive your greatest satisfaction.

In the early chapters you were asked to spend a significant amount of time creating the foundation components of your PRP. The intent was to establish some clarity between you and your partner about what you both want and need in your retirement years. If you and your partner work through the suggested foundations steps, you will not only understand each other better but you will also begin to communicate more effectively with one another. The process is not driven by financial concerns; rather it is driven by the desire to communicate your true feelings and expectations about retirement.

This is an instance where the "process" of planning your retirement is as important as the actual plan itself.

The creation of your PRP represents one of the best opportunities that a couple will have to improve their relationship. Those couples who already have a fantastic relationship will be able to enhance and expand their relationship. Those couples, who have drifted apart, for whatever the reason, can use the planning process as an opportunity to rebuild a relationship. After all, you and your spouse or partner will be spending the rest of your lives together. You might as well make your retirement years the best years of your life.

An Example: Marriage Encounter

There is a popular program for married couples called "Marriage Encounter." The program is designed to bring married couples closer together emotionally, psychologically and physically regardless of the quality of their existing marriage. One of the techniques they use is to have each spouse spend quiet personal time separately as they contemplate their relationship and then express their feelings by writing a letter to the other spouse about such topics as money, children, religion, sex, work, health, death, etc. Then the couple comes back together and reads each other's letters. The discussion that follows has helped many thousands of couples to improve the quality of their relationship. The key was their ability to learn and understand the inner feelings of the other partner about the status of their relationship.

I believe a similar thing is needed as the catalyst to bring couples together in retirement planning. I don't imply that all couples have drifted apart and must first reunite; rather I suggest that years of focus on career and family may have created a bit of a complacency or take-it-for-granted attitude with regards to the interpersonal relationship. The key to happiness in retirement is to get both partners to understand each other's true needs and feelings as they enter the culminating years of their relationship with one another.

When you exchanged vows with your partner on your wedding day, you had your entire life ahead of you to fulfill your vows. Now many decades later you might need another exchange of vows that will allow you to recommit to your relationship as a requirement for entering the retirement or culminating years of the relationship. The creation of your PRP provides you with the opportunity.

If you put financial planning at the front of your retirement planning, you might miss a tremendous opportunity to establish a new and improved relationship with your partner. After all, there is much more to life and personal fulfillment than money.

My purpose for including financial planning and integration in your overall PRP is to ensure that you do, in fact, seek out competent and qualified financial planners to guide you in creating the financial component of your PRP. You can't ignore the importance of adequate financial planning but you also can't allow the financial plan to dominate everything else in your PRP. Regardless of your financial condition, you must still find a way to maximize your resources so that you can get done all the things you want and need to do in order to achieve your life goals for satisfaction and personal fulfillment.

It would not be appropriate to recommend a particular financial planning approach or firm or individual, but there are a few myths about financial planning that tend to get in the way of the financial aspects of retirement planning.

Myth #1: There is One Size-Fits-All Financial Plan

Financial planning is like trying to compare people. It can't be done. We are all different. We have different needs and circumstances. Therefore, there is no one best financial plan or planning approach. Similarly there is no one best investment or investment strategy that works for everyone. Financial planning is clearly a situation in which you have to cut the cloth to fit the person. The only way to find the right financial planner is to talk with several of them and evaluate their recommendations based on the quality and appropriateness of their plan. Be sure to get several references from long-term clients. Never commit to a long-term relationship until you are convinced that they are able to deliver on their promises.

Myth #2: Financial Planning is only for the Wealthy

One of the great misconceptions about financial planning is that it is a requirement for only the wealthy. Although the wealthy may have larger tax and estate issues, the smaller and medium size investors stand more to lose if they make a poor decision about where to put their money. A wealthy person may risk a million dollars on a risky venture with the realization that it will not jeopardize their total estate. A smaller investor might not be able to afford to gamble on their nest egg. The quality of investment advice is just as important to the small investor as it is to the big investor. However, the little investors represent the bulk of retirees and financial planners usually do not need to spend a great amount of time coming up with a quality financial plan. If you don't have a huge investment portfolio, you should not avoid financial planning. No investor, regardless of the size of their investment portfolio, can afford the potential tax and estate implications for failing to plan the short and long term implications of their money.

Myth #3: Live Frugally and Save for the Future

The amount of money you spend in your retirement is dependent on two things: the size of your retirement fund and your personal attitude about spending money. If you have a lot of money and don't need to watch what you spend, you may never experience the frustrations of debt or the worries about unexpected expenses. If you have a limited retirement fund, you obviously have to live within a budget to help ensure that your funds last through your lifetime. But sadly there are frugal people, rich and not so rich, who practice frugality as if it were a virtue. You will get no more points in Heaven by dying with an excess of money. If you are so preoccupied with saving for the future, it is possible that you might avoid doing things in the present that you should do to enjoy life. The thing that is really important is whether or not you used your assets, personal and financial, to benefit your family and others who are less fortunate. There are many wealthy people who are eccentric about spending money but they should be judged not on the amount of money they spend or their possessions but what they spend it on. You may recall that when Sam Walton was alive he drove an old pickup truck to work, but he gave millions of dollars to charity.

Myth #4: Financial Planning Starts Near Retirement

One of the big issues in financial planning is when should you start to plan for retirement. Some people think that they have to get through the early stages of their family and career before they start thinking about money and retirement. The ideal time to start planning for retirement is when you start working. The logic is that your financial plan starts when you start earning money. If you don't develop sound saving and investment goals early in your career, you will be put in the situation of having to play catch-up later on. If you wait until after the kids are out of college and the mortgage is paid off, you might not have enough income or time to create an adequate retirement nest egg. The best time to start planning for retirement is when you begin your career.

Myth #5: The Size of the Estate Determines Retirement Strategy

The size of your retirement fund is only one of the issues that will determine your retirement wants and needs. If you have a large retirement fund, it may be easier to make decisions about working or traveling or buying things or giving to charity, but the size of your retirement fund should not prevent you from doing things that you really want to do. For instance, if you really want to travel in your retirement, you can do it either first class on a personal jet or tourist class in your automobile. The important point is that you should plan what you want to do in retirement before you determine how much it will cost. Obviously a person with a small retirement fund can't plan on things like a second home for the winter season, but they might be able to find an inexpensive rental or even camp out at a state park. If there is a will, there is a way. If you allow money to determine your level of happiness, you will quickly become bitter and disillusioned. Money does not buy happiness. If you doubt that, consider all of the many lottery winners who are leading miserable lives. Money will only make you happy if you are happy with yourself and you use your money to enhance your satisfaction and fulfillment.

Myth #6: Retirement Planning Should Focus on the Long Range

Some people become more consumed with what they will leave their heirs than what they will do with their money while they are still alive. Money is for the living. Those who are fortunate to have a lot of money also have a larger responsibility to use their money wisely and compassionately. The people with huge estates may use financial planners to help them maximize the size of the estate for their heirs. I read recently that one of the richest men in the world had advised his children that he intends to give the great bulk of his multi-billion dollar estate to charity. His children will receive enough money to help them jumpstart their careers but not enough money so that they no longer have a need to work. It is unlikely you will find any of his heirs corrupted by a windfall of money that they did not earn. The key point is that retirement planning should focus on your personal wants and needs while you are able to enjoy life and the satisfactions that come from helping those who are less fortunate. If you have a relatively modest retirement fund, you should build your financial plan to last your expected life span and if there is not enough money then you determine the anticipated shortfall and create a viable plan that will allow you to earn additional money. There are lots of seniors that have created successful new careers in their retirement years. One notable example was Colonel Sanders who created Kentucky Fried Chicken when he was in his retirement years. If he had simply tried to live on his small retirement fund, it is likely he would not have enjoyed life or taken the initiative to earn additional money.

The bottom line for his chapter is the need for you to create your financial plan as an integrated component of your master PRP, not as a stand-alone process.

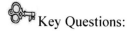 Key Questions:

- Do you have a qualified financial planner and advisor?
- Will your advisor be available during your retirement years?
- Do you have an up-to-date financial plan?
- Does your financial plan have to be adjusted to compensate for changes in your retirement plans?
- If your financial nest egg is not projected to be large enough to cover you and your partner's life expectancy, what are your plans to make up for the shortfall?
- In the event of an unplanned financial burden that could wipe out a substantial amount of your financial nest egg, do you have a contingency or fall back plan?

Chapter 18

How to Start Your Personalized Retirement Plan

*"The only thing that holds a marriage together is the husband bein'
big enough to keep his mouth shut, to step back and see where his wife
is wrong."*   ~Archie Bunker in "All in the Family"

Now that you've read the Ten Steps you are ready to close the loop by
completing your own Personalized Retirement Plan.

The process of beginning your PRP is similar to other major event in
your life. You simply have to sit down and get started. I recall clearly
how I developed my plan to ask my future wife to marry me. I
rehearsed in my mind how it would all come together. I asked her
father for permission. I planned the right setting, the right moment,
and the right words. I built up my courage to avoid the nervousness
and to have the conviction and determination to actually do it.

The engagement process then opened the door to the next really big
planning opportunity; namely, planning the wedding. Sit back quietly
and think about what you and your spouse, and family, went through
in planning and organizing your wedding, whether is it was a huge
ceremony or private affair. The process of what you went through way
back then is similar to what you will face when you start your
retirement planning process.

It may have been a very long time since you and your partner have sat
down together and developed a plan. There is a point in a relationship
where both partners tend to operate on well ingrained habit patterns.
Both of you are so familiar with the tendencies of each other that you
sometimes operate instinctively. You may not ask for an opinion, you
simply do it because you assume that you know what the other partner
wants or expects. But, retirement poses a new challenge. It represents

uncharted territory. You can't just plunge in and trust your prior experience because you have no experience with retirement.

You are at this point in the book because you have already made a commitment to develop a retirement plan. It is important that you abandon your ingrained habit patterns in which you believe you understand your partner implicitly. You need to start with a clean sheet of paper and with an open mind about each of the ten planning steps.

The purpose of this chapter is to help you get started, in the right way. Below you will find a step by step process to help you get started, but first let me give you a few tips.

First, it is absolutely necessary that both partners read this book. During the first reading, it is not necessary to stop and answer all the questions. Simply read the book so you understand what you will be discussing. This must be a mutual process, not a one-sided or preconceived self-fulfilling prophecy about what one partner wants.

Second, planning is a process, not a single event. There is no set schedule for the number of times you sit down and plan, nor is there any time limit on how long it should take. The important thing is that you spend as much time as is necessary to make sure both of you are on the same page.

Third, the process of planning your retirement is as important as the resulting retirement plan. You can't arrive at your personalized retirement plan without engaging each other in highly personal and detailed discussions. The goal is to listen, really listen, to each other and come to a mutual consensus on specific issues. But, don't move to the next step until you have honest agreement on each issue.

Fourth, when you arrive at a mutual agreement on the important issues, the byproduct will be a sense of commitment to work your plan based on your mutual agreement. There is always a better result when two people are committed to the same goal. Think about how difficult it would be if one partner dominates the discussion and decides to move to Florida while the other partner desires strongly to stay in the current homestead. How happy will this couple be in retirement?

Setting the Stage

There are a few things you should discuss in advance of your first meeting that will help to organize the process.

Determine Who Will Lead the Process—each relationship usually has one partner who takes the lead in major family or interpersonal discussions. You need to determine which partner will take the lead in running the administrative side of creating your PRP. This does not imply in any way that the other partner will take a secondary role. Rather the whole intent of the process is to develop a mutual, cooperative spirit that results in a plan that represents the thinking and feelings of both partners. The role of the designated leader is to guide the process and maintain the necessary written materials.

Schedule an appointment—start by scheduling a date and time for your first and subsequent planning meetings. Although the total process should not be rigid or highly structured, the idea of scheduling your meetings is important because it elevates the significance and importance of the event. For instance, during your business or professional career you would routinely schedule important meetings to make sure the date was secure and that you provided the other party with the opportunity to get prepared for the meeting. Since your retirement planning is one of the most important events in your life, it makes sense to formalize your first meeting.

Determine where to meet—I highly recommend that you schedule your meetings at a time and place where you can guarantee several hours of uninterrupted privacy. No public places, no phones, no one else present, no TV, no alcoholic drinks. Just the two of you in a nice quiet, relaxed environment.

Take Notes--determine who will take notes during your meetings. Again, don't make it too formal, but keep in mind that you will be discussing some very important and personal issues and you want to capture and preserve them while they are fresh in your minds. The planning record will also serve as a reminder and reference point as you go down the path of retirement. You want to avoid potential conflicts later on when one or the other party questions the goals and desires expressed during your initial meetings.

The planning record can be a simple notebook or a comprehensive binder depending on the desires and style of each partner. You can use the summary of key questions in Chapter 20—Personalized Retirement Plan Workbook and jot your responses right in the book. You might also want to consider creating a "retirement scrapbook" with the first chapter being your Personalized Retirement Plan. Then you can update the scrapbook periodically with the exciting and interesting events that occur in your retirement.

Initiate a Mutual Dialog—the use of a mutual dialog is absolutely necessary. Each partner should express their point of view on all questions. You need to be very open and honest. This is not the time to hold back. This is the time to really communicate. Express your true feelings not what you think your partner wants to hear. Don't be afraid that you might offend or disappoint. After all, retirement is the culmination of your life so if you have held back your feelings in the past, now is the time to be up front and honest.

Keep in mind that a dialog is a two-way street. Both partners have to express their feelings and thoughts. If not, you will end up with a plan that half of the team might not believe in or support.

Communication is a Two Way Street
I recall an incident that illustrates the difficulty of trying to establish true communication. It involved a personal conversation I had with one of our sons a long time ago. Here is how the story unfolded...*I thought it was time that we sat down and talked about the birds and bees. After a few aborted attempts, I finally got my thoughts together and we went out for a drive during which I explained in appropriate detail how things worked. I waxed on eloquently while my son listened intently, never asking a question. I didn't ask him any questions either because he seemed to be getting the message. The more I talked, the more confident I got and the more silent he became. None the less, I thought that I had done a rather remarkable job of explaining a rather complex subject. When I was finished, I beamed at my newly educated son and asked if he had any questions, any questions at all, man to man. He paused, looked at me pensively and asked, "Dad, who do you think will go to the World Series this year?"*

Moral: Just because you are talking to someone doesn't mean that you are actually communicating.

The spirit of your communication is extremely important. You should develop a mutual dialog, not a monologue or something dominated by one of the partners. For instance, if one partner has traditionally been a stronger personality, now is the time for that partner to spend a lot of time listening to the other partner. Sometimes the partner who was the primary "bread winner" tends to take a more dominant position on what he or she wants to do in retirement. If that occurs, simply write down your desires and treat it as one alternative, then allow the other partner to express their feelings. You might be surprised what the other partner really thinks.

For instance, my wife and partner of over 40 years expressed to me during our planning sessions that she felt somewhat unfulfilled in one area of her life since she was not able to have an independent working career. Although she was a trained and registered nurse, she did not have the opportunity to create her own career because she became a "stay-at-home mom". Although in my mind I thought she had experienced a wonderful and rewarding career, in her mind she felt something was missing. Therefore, it became extremely important that she be able to express her desires to do something in her retirement that would allow her to experience the satisfaction of having an independent career.

Key point: Don't assume you know the inner most thoughts of your partner regardless of how long you have lived with him or her.

Another important point: when a partner really opens up and expresses their thoughts or feelings that may have been suppressed for many years, it is absolutely imperative that the other partner not use the occasion to critique or disagree or find fault. The intent is to have open communication, not to conform to one partner's point of view. It is okay to ask for clarification but you should not attempt to change a partner's feelings. You can disagree with facts but feelings are personal and intuitive. When a partner says, "I can't help it that is the way I feel." The other partner has to simply accept and respect the right of the other partner to have that feeling.

If you or your partner are not able to engage in a mutual dialog or you are preoccupied with other issues, then stop the process and try to determine why you are not able to communicate with one another. If you can't resolve the issues with each other, you should seek professional help. There is too much at stake to slip back into a psychological roadblock that might jeopardize your retirement.

In advance of the first meeting, each partner should review the questions and jot down some notes to insure that you don't forget any

---

important issues. It may take anywhere from a few hours to several days to organize your thoughts. Don't rush yourself. Take as much time as necessary to dig deep into your inner self to answer all of the questions. If you are not able to answer some questions because you are not sure or haven't really thought about it, that's okay, just jot down your thoughts so you can discuss them with your partner.

When and Where to Start?

"The man who goes alone can start today; but he who travels with another must wait till that other is ready."

~Henry David Thoreau

The answer to the first question, "When to start?" is simple: get started when you are ready to start planning for your retirement. For some people it is in their 50s, for others it is in their 60s. The fact that you bought this book is a pretty good indication that you are ready to begin preparing a retirement game plan.

Whether you are several years away from retirement or are in the final countdown to retirement, you can begin the process by developing preliminary responses to the key questions in Chapters 9-18. I say "preliminary" because you don't want to develop your final responses until you and your partner have a chance to discuss each question. It is vital that you express your true feelings and not succumb to pressure in order to avoid a potential conflict. You will be living with your decisions for a very long time so make sure both of you are on the same page. Once you are in agreement, you can start to write down your responses.

If you are years away from retirement, keep in mind that some of your responses might change for lots of reasons that you are not able to anticipate when you started the dialog. For instance, earlier in my career I felt very strongly that I was going to retire when I turned 55. But when I celebrated my 55th birthday I realized that I was at the peak of my capabilities and earning potential and I really loved what I was doing so I advanced my retirement goal to age 60. Then when I got to age 60, an age that when I was 30 was perceived to be ancient, I once again realized that I was not that old after all. When I got to 60, I advanced it again to 65. There is no magic about particular ages. What is really important is that you have a desire to retire. If it never comes, don't worry about it, just keep on doing what you are doing.

Impact of Change

It is okay to be fluid, dynamic and flexible with your retirement plan. It is always subject to change as conditions change, but it is far better to change a plan than to have no plan at all. The other issue that becomes a reality as we age is that our attitudes and feelings change. At one time in your life you might have dreamed of a quaint little cottage on the beach as your retirement nirvana. Years later you might see a need to be closer to an aging parent or a child or grandchild who needs tender loving care. The point is that things change and you can adjust your retirement plan accordingly.

The second question deals with how to get started. The best way to start the process is to go to the workbook in Chapter 20 and begin your dialog by answering the "conversation starter" questions followed by the "key questions" which are summarized from Chapters 9-18 (the Ten Steps for creating your PRP).

Once you start your dialog, you are officially involved in the process of creating your personalized retirement plan.

Don't Forget about Financial Planning

Regardless of when you start the retirement planning process, it is very important that you don't wait until retirement to start your financial planning. You need to initiate a savings and investment program very early in your career to provide the funds that will form the foundation for your retirement nest egg. The sequence of events tends to follow a pattern for most retirees:

- Early to Mid-Career—focus on creating a savings and investment program that would be earmarked for retirement. Select a financial planner.
- Late Career—begin the process to prepare your retirement plan.
- Pre-Retirement—finalize your personalized retirement plan and integrate your retirement financial plan into your retirement plan.
- Retirement—implement your retirement plan.

Planning Exceptions

An important issue that needs to be considered is what happens if you are single, or you lost your spouse or partner, or you have a long lapse between the start and completion of your plan. Below are some helpful suggestions.

Single Partners—if you are single, divorced or living without a partner, you should still create your PRP. The process of planning for the future is just as important for singles as it is for couples. Singles might want to select a very close relative or friend to review and validate their plan to make sure it fits their style and personality.

Lost Partner—if you have lost a cherished partner you should view yourself as a "single" and do your best to complete your PRP. You will probably instinctively imagine how your former partner might have answered the questions. Regardless of how long you were with your former partner, their legacy will affect your retirement planning directly or indirectly for many years into the future, so don't ignore it. They will be in your mind and hearts in your retirement anyway.

Lapse in Planning—life is dynamic and things can happen that interrupt your planning process. If you are not able to complete your retirement plan, just put it on the shelf and pick it up at a later date. The quality of your responses will still be relevant at some future date; all you have to do is review and update them. The important point is that you should not abandon your retirement plan entirely once you've started the process.

Once you have completed the initial questions and you are still able to communicate with each other, you might want to reflect on your answers for a few days. You should schedule your next meeting in a week or so to confirm or add some additional thoughts that were triggered during your first meeting. If you are okay with your answers, put them in your notebook or scrapbook and move to the next step.

It is extremely important that you write down your answers to all questions. They will become the principal components of your PRP and will be used for reference in the future.

It is likely that your initial dialog may have created a new sense of togetherness because it brought you together to talk about issues that you may not have discussed for many years. You are now ready to start implementing your retirement plan and enjoying your new found relationship.

Chapter 19

Personalized Retirement Plan Workbook

"Good plans shape good decisions. That's why good planning helps to make elusive dreams come true."

~ Lester Robert Bittel, Writer

This chapter is a summary of the 🔑 Key Questions that were listed at the end of the chapters detailing the Ten Steps (for creating your Personalized Retirement Plan). You can use this section as a workbook for finalizing your responses or you can copy each of the questions and your responses to a separate notebook or computer.

Begin Your Dialog with Conversation Starters

If you delayed writing your responses to the questions, no problem, you can use this section to start the dialog with your partner. The initial questions below are suggested conversation starters. The purpose is to transform your thought process from your normal "work a day" world into a future state in which you share your inner most thoughts and feelings with your partner. Remember: there is no "right" or "wrong" responses, only your personal responses.

- How do you feel about retiring? Happy? Sad? Confused? Eager? Reluctant? Don't know yet?
- Do you really want to retire? Want to keep working? Full or part-time?
- Do you still need to continue working because of financial concerns?
- Would you like to use your skills, experience and wisdom to do something else? A new career?

- What is the single most important thing that you want to do or see happen to you and your partner in retirement?
- Are you ready to discuss your feelings and thoughts about retirement planning? If not, why not?
- Are you convinced that you need to have more than a financial plan to guide and monitor your retirement experience?
- What are your biggest concerns or fears about retirement?
- What has been your most significant accomplishment in your life to date?
- What has been your greatest disappointment in your life to date?
- Describe your ideal retirement.
- Have you achieved a state of fulfillment in your life? If not, what do you still need to do?
- If money was not an issue, what would you do in your retirement?
- How will you replace the stimulation and satisfaction that your job or career provided?
- How will you and your partner adjust to being together for longer periods of time every day? Will you inadvertently get in each other's way?
- What are the things that you worry about if you were to pass away suddenly?
- Have you discussed your feelings about life without each other? Practical and family issues? Remarriage?

Now that you are warmed up to the task of answering penetrating questions, it's time to get started on the Key Questions imbedded within the Ten Steps (Chapters 9-18). The purpose of the Key Questions is to identify the core issues that create the foundation for your PRP. Below is a summary of the Ten Steps and the Key Questions.

Step 1—Wants and Needs

 Work:

- Do you still *need* to work? What is your plan?
- Do you still *want* to work? What is your plan?

 Family Relationships:

- What family relationships do you *want* to improve or maintain?
- What family relationships do you *need* to improve or maintain?

 Social Relationships:

- Do you *need* to or *want* to re-establish or improve any social relationships or friendships?

 Religion:

- Do you *want or need* to make any changes in your views on church or the role of religion in your life?

 Community:

- What do you *need* to do within my community that might make a difference for someone less fortunate?
- What community organizations do you *want* to get involved in?

Step 2—Obligations and Commitments

 Family

- Do you have obligations or commitments with parents, children or grandchildren that will influence your retirement plan?
- How will you deal with these issues when you can no longer fulfill your obligation?

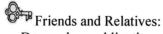 Friends and Relatives:
- Do you have obligations or commitments to friends or relatives that will impact your retirement plans?
- Who are the friends and relatives that you want to stay close to during retirement?

Business and Professional Relationships:
- Do you have on-going business or professional obligations or commitments to consider that will influence your retirement plan?
- Are there any business or professional relationships or friendships that need to be addressed?

Organizations:
- Do you have any obligations, commitments or preferences involving social or civic organizations or clubs that will affect your retirement plan?
- Have you considered your partner when evaluating your obligations and commitments to these organizations and clubs?

Church and Religion Relationships:
- Are there obligations or commitments that involve your church or religion that might affect your retirement plan?

Community Relationships:
- Do you have community or political obligations, commitments or desires that you need to consider in developing your retirement plan?

Step 3—Personal Inventory

 Strengths, Weaknesses, Opportunities, Threats:

- What are your strengths?
- What is your greatest strength or your underlying core competency?
- What are your weaknesses?
- What opportunities are there that you want to capitalize on?
- Are there issues or threats that need to be resolved or avoided?

Step 4—Life after Retirement

 Key Questions:

- Are both of you psychologically, emotionally and financially ready for retirement?
- What is your attitude about retirement? Your partner?
- Do you have enough money to retire or will you need to continue working full or part-time?
- Is retirement your decision or is it being imposed on you?
- Will you be able to cope with the loss of career and the recognition and rewards you got from it?
- Do you want to stop or merely slow down?
- Are there alternatives to retirement? A new career?

Step 5—Goals and Fulfillment

 Goals and Fulfillment:

- What are the primary accomplishments in your career and life?
- What personal goals did you establish for yourself?

- If you didn't have specific goals, describe the condition or set of circumstances that will make you feel happy and content in retirement.
- What personal goals do you still want to accomplish in retirement?
- What will provide you with a true sense of satisfaction and personal fulfillment?
- What would you like your legacy to be" How do you want to be remembered?

Step 6—Physical Conditioning

 Key Questions:

- Do you have any physical issues that might impact your retirement plan?
- When will you schedule a routine physical exam with your doctor to identify any potential issues that need to be addressed?
- Have you and your doctor developed your key physical indicators (KPI)?
- What are your improvement targets for each key physical indicator?
- What specific actions will you take to improve your physical indicators?
- What is your plan for smoking, excess drinking, over the counter drug dependence?
- What is your plan for developing a healthy diet?
- Are there other physical issues that you don't need to do but that you want to do something about?
- When will you start?

Step 7—Mental Conditioning

 Key Questions:

- Do you plan to engage in any formal or informal learning program like adult education, continuous learning or distance learning?
- What specific activities will you engage in regularly and routinely to maintain and improve the condition of your brain? Reading? Writing? Painting? Music? Hobbies? Cards? Chess? Board games? Crossword puzzles? Sudoku? Part-time work? Volunteering?

Step 8—Lifestyle, Leisure and Location

 Key Questions:

- How would you describe your current lifestyle?
- What do you like about your lifestyle? Your partner?
- What don't you like? Your partner?
- Are you content to continue your current lifestyle in retirement? Any lifestyle changes? Why?
- Where do you want to live in retirement? Why?
- Where will you live when you might need assistance?
- What leisure activities do you want to pursue? To what extent? Your partner?
- How much of your time do you want to devote to leisure? How much to work? Volunteering? Personal development?
- What is your ideal balance between all activities? Your partner?
- Have you compared all of the characteristics of a new potential location? Weather? Traffic? Healthcare? Cultural and social activities? Crime? Cost of Living? Impact of family, friends, church and community? Support network? Professional relationships? Compatibility?

Step 9—Exit Strategy

 Estate Planning Issues:

- ❑ Do you and your partner have an up-to-date last will and testament?
- ❑ Do you have an attorney who understands your will and requirements? Will your attorney be available during our retirement years?
- ❑ Have you prepared Advanced Directives (living will, medical power of attorney, and do not resuscitate orders) that spell out what you want done in the event you are incapacitated?
- ❑ Do you have a power of attorney document that specifies who is legally allowed to make decisions in your behalf?
- ❑ Have you determined, or updated, your executor, administrator and trustee for handling the details your last will and testament?

 Personal Requirements:

- ❑ Have you had an "exit discussion" with your spouse, partner and family members to advise them of your wishes after you are deceased?
- ❑ Have you discussed and written down your funeral wishes? Where? Formal, informal, private, public? Who officiates? Pall bearers? Eulogists? Hymns? Prayers? Post-funeral reception and arrangements?
- ❑ Have you written or provided your family with the highlights of your obituary?
- ❑ Have you specified your burial wishes? Where? Cremation? Burial?
- ❑ Have you determined if you want a headstone? The inscription?

Step 10—Integrate Financial Plans

Key Questions:

❏ Do you have a qualified financial planner and advisor?
❏ Will your advisor be available during your retirement years?
❏ Do you have an up-to-date financial plan?
❏ Does your financial plan have to be adjusted to compensate for changes in your retirement plans?
❏ If your financial nest egg is not projected to be large enough to cover you and your partner's life expectancy, what are your plans to make up for the shortfall?
❏ In the event of an unplanned financial burden that could wipe out a substantial amount of your financial nest egg, do you have a contingency or fall back plan?

Completing Your Personalized Retirement Game Plan

You have worked very hard to get to this point; the next steps will help you complete your PRP.

1. Organize Your Notes—go back and collect the answers to the Conversation Starter Questions and the Ten Steps. These questions helped you start your dialog but also contain valuable information about your hopes and intentions for retirement.

2. Steps 1-10—the answers to the Key Questions are the source you will use to summarize a checklist of the key actions you need to implement and monitor to complete your PRP.

3. Implementation and Monitoring—read the next chapter for helpful hints on how to implement and monitor your PRP.

Chapter 20

Implementing and Monitoring Your Personalized Retirement Plan

"In preparing for battle I have always found that plans are useless, but planning is indispensable."

~General Dwight D. Eisenhauer

Once you have developed your Personalized Retirement Plan (PRP), you have two more steps to accomplish. First, you have to start to implement the plan; second, you need to put in place a process that allows you to follow-up and monitor the plan. The best laid plans mean nothing unless they are executed well and monitored to ensure that the goals are achieved.

Some of the best examples of successful plans are those created by military leaders like Alexander the Great, Hannibal, George Washington, Ulysses S. Grant, Dwight Eisenhauer, George Patton, Douglas MacArthur, Norman Schwartzkopf and many others. One of the characteristics of a good military plan is the contingent strategy or what happens if something goes wrong? For instance, the invasion of Normandy in World War II was probably the largest military plan in the history of warfare due to the magnitude and depth of the contingency plans. The key to victory or success is to incorporate a monitoring capability into the plan that tracks and evaluates performance.

The same is similar for retirement planning. There is a need to incorporate a monitoring mechanism that helps you manage the process and react to changing conditions. You can't anticipate everything and the PRP is not intended to become a "written in stone" document. It is merely an aid to help you achieve your retirement goals.

At this stage of your discussions you should have a much better understanding about your partner's thoughts and feelings about retirement. In addition, you should feel good about your meetings and the things you discussed. Hopefully you will also sense that you are beginning to communicate more effectively than you did previously.

Below are the things you need to consider in creating your monitoring plan.

1. **Develop a checklist**—the foundation component of your PRP is only a plan. It is not yet a completed action. You need to go back over the notes you took and prepare a checklist of all the proposed actions. Simply describe the action and write down the name of the responsible partner.

2. **Establish priorities**—next you should use the checklist to develop priorities and specific completion dates. The priority setting is important because both of you will have quite a lot of things you need to do and you can't do all of them immediately. Determine the relative importance from top to bottom and develop your respective priorities. It is also important to establish a specific completion date so you can have a means to manage your time and to help insure that you won't let some actions drag on and on. Suggestion: establish your priority using two guidelines. First, use a numerical ranking to determine the relative priority. For instance, the number "1" is the highest priority; the number "3" is the lowest priority; the number "2" is somewhere in the middle. Second, use an approximate time line to determine when something needs to be done. For instance, if it needs to be done is 3 months or less, assign a letter "a"; 3 to 6 months gets a "b"; 6 months or beyond is a "c".

In summary, if one of your action points is listed as "1a" it means that it is the highest priority and needs to be done in less than 3 months. A "3c" is the lowest priority with a target of 6 months or more. You will quickly learn to understand the priority approach.

The last step is to put the name of the responsible partner next to the action. The finished checklist will identify all the action points with a priority and the name of the responsible partner.

3. **Schedule a routine follow-up meeting**—once you have established your priorities, the next step is to decide when and how you will monitor and follow-up your planned actions. I suggest that during your first year of retirement you establish a monthly follow-up meeting to discuss and review the status of your combined actions. You might want to consider something as simple as using your anniversary day as the monthly meeting date. For instance, if you were married on June 15, the 15th of each month is your assigned meeting date.

Key Point: remember that an important goal of your PRP was to establish *effective communication*. The routine follow-ups are a tool to help you communicate more effectively. In addition, the meetings will be a constant reminder of your commitment to each other and your PRP.

You should meet monthly during your first full year of retirement, or at the commencement of your retirement planning. Then you can consider backing off to every other month or quarterly and eventually a semi-annually if your retirement is working well.

4. **Commit to the plan**—both partners must commit to the monitoring plan to ensure that you actually use it to implement your PRP. There will always be other things that will compete for your time, as you get active in your retirement years. You need to promise each other that your PRP is the most important thing that you need to do.

For instance, a loving partner never forgets a wedding anniversary or birthday because the dates have taken on a major significance in your lives. You need to approach the monitoring plan with the same intensity to make sure you don't discard your PRP once the meetings have become routine.

5. **Conduct an annual audit**—just like companies conduct an annual audit of their books, it is suggested that you review your accomplishments on the anniversary of your PRP each year. The intent of the meeting is to take a broader look at your PRP than you do during your monthly review meetings. The reality is that things change. There is no way to predict the future, all you can do is to plan as best you can and then adjust or react to unanticipated changes.

    For instance, a health crisis might sidetrack plans. Or, a financial windfall might change your thinking about your expenses or where you might want to live. Or, a new job or hobby or activity might open up a new opportunity that might change your time plans. Or an event like a natural disaster might alter the landscape, literally, of your home or belongings. Think about the impact of the hurricanes in Florida and the impact it had on the lives of thousands of retirees.

    Key Point: when unexpected events happen that alter your PRP, just rework that part of your plan, and don't abandon the total plan. If you had prior experience in creating and implementing annual business or organization plans, you realize that a plan is simply a plan, not a guarantee of a result. You simply adjust and move on.

    The suggested approach for conducting your annual audit is to use your checklist as a guide in reviewing the overall status of your planned actions.

6. **Maintain the perspective**—there is a prevailing belief that the primary role of a CEO in a business or the head of any organization, including a mother or father, is to *maintain the perspective*. The implication is that people can be easily distracted by events happening around them and lose track of the original intent or purpose of what they were supposed to be doing. Like the classic maxim, "When you're up to your backside in alligators, it's hard to remember that the original purpose of the exercise was to drain the swamp." Many times in life we lose sight of the original purpose of our actions and dwell on the symptoms rather than the root causes.

Each partner needs to put the PRP and planning process into its proper perspective. Your PRP is simply a tool to use in helping you organize and implement your retirement goals and desires. You have not created your PRP in order to have a plan, rather the purpose behind the plan is to improve the probability that you will enjoy retirement and achieve satisfaction and ultimately your personal fulfillment.

The monitoring plan is an important step that is intended to help you manage your PRP on a regular, routine basis. Be sure to keep it simple but remember that the ultimate success of your PRP is not your planning skills but your commitment to communicate and to do the things you planned.

Section Three

Insights and Words of Wisdom

"Knowledge comes, but wisdom lingers. It may not be difficult to store up in the mind a vast quantity of facts within a comparatively short time, but the ability to form judgments requires the severe discipline of hard work and the tempering heat of experience and maturity."

~Calvin Coolidge, President

Chapter 21

Retirement Planning Insights

"Don't simply retire from something; have something to retire to."
~Harry Emerson Fosdick

There are many millions of retirees who have gone before you and left behind some valuable insights about how to prepare for retirement. You have the advantage of learning from their successes and failures. After talking to many retirees and sorting through their responses, I summarized their observations and recommendations into ten insights. They are presented below as guidelines to help you start your retirement planning process. You would be wise to take advantage of this condensed experience and wisdom.

The number of insights happened to represent the same number of steps that are in the Personalized Retirement Plan. These insights are not related to the ten steps in the PRP but will prepare you for getting into the PRP process.

❑ **Retirement Perspective**—you need to establish the proper perspective about retirement because it is important that you understand what you are getting into. Perhaps the most important perspective is that *you are in charge of your retirement planning.* You literally control when you retire, where you retire, what you do with your time, or whether or not you actually retire.

No one is going to peer over your shoulder and tell you what to do; it's your call. Keep in mind that *retirement is an option, your option, not a necessity.* You should retire only when you want to retire, not when someone, or some rule or company guideline, tells you to retire. If you want to retire from your job, fine, no problem. If you want to continue working, fine, no problem. If you want to work part-time or start a new career, that's fine too.

You are the boss. Of course, if your company or institution has rules about when you should retire, you will have to discuss your intentions and determine the best course of action.

Things were a whole lot different when your parents retired. Back then it was an expected occurrence. Everybody retired eventually. Retirement was a traditional event. Your parents got the proverbial gold watch and some type of pension. Then they lived happily ever after.

Not so these days. Retirement is now more of an option for you to consider. Granted there are still lots of soon-to-be-retired who are counting the days until they can shut off the alarm clock, roll over and dream about what they are going to do.

There is also a very large contingent of seniors who will continue to work, some because of financial necessity and some because they still enjoy their work. There is nothing wrong with making a decision to postpone retirement or put it on the back burner. Or, to retire from your present job and go into a new career or activity. Think of it as an emerging Retirement Renaissance. Your first task in planning your retirement is to develop the appropriate perspective about retirement. Whatever you do is up to you.

Some potential retirees may want to eat their cake and have it too. One way to do that is to cut back a little on your work schedule and devote your newfound time to other things you would like to do. There is nothing wrong with that.

A business friend of mine had a unique way of retiring; he retired one day at a time. First, he took off Mondays and worked four days; then he took off Fridays and worked three days; eventually he got his work schedule down to one or two days that were compatible with the amount of time he wanted to devote to work.

There are more and more companies and institutions that are happy to have their senior people stay on the job with a reduced time commitment. After all, you have developed a huge amount of experience and wisdom that the younger generation will take years to develop. Remember that your experience and wisdom is a valuable asset to your organization. For instance, if you add up the total value of your compensation and benefits over the course of your career, the resulting figure is one way to estimate your true value. Example: if your compensation and benefits totaled $75,000 a year for 30 years, the value that you represent as an asset to your organization is $2,250,000. When you walk out the door, the organization will have to replace this asset. You might be in a position to negotiate a tremendous deal to work part-time with a handsome financial incentive so your organization can preserve and use this valuable asset.

The perspective you need to have as you begin the retirement planning process is that you should not rule out any options. You should consider doing things that you really enjoy, even if it involves making no changes at all.

❑ **Commitment to Plan**--as the old saying goes, "If you don't know where you are going, how will you know when you get there?" You must make a commitment to prepare a Personalized Retirement Plan. The problem with working without a PRP is that time is not on your side. If you still have lots of things you want to do, and that describes most potential retirees, you don't have an infinite amount of time to waste.

By the time most people retire, they are into the "last quarter" of the game of life. Reality suggests that you will have ten or twenty or possibly 30 years to enjoy your retirement dreams. About 13% of the seniors over 65 will reach the magical age of 100. In 2005 there were 55,000 centenarians in the United States population. The numbers indicate that 87% of all seniors will pass to the great beyond before they reach 100. Regardless of how old you become, the best way to accomplish all your goals is to develop a PRP, establish your priorities, and get started.

If you want to live happily ever after, literally, you must make a commitment to develop a PRP. The first step in developing you plan is to start talking to your planning partner or family about your retirement goals.

❑ **Mutual Planning Approach**—if you are married, or have a significant other, you must, I repeat, you **must** develop a **mutual** approach to retirement planning. If you were the primary breadwinner in your home, you might tend to think that retirement is only about you. Wrong. Your spouse or significant other must be a part of the process or you are likely to run aground when you begin to do your thing and your partner has other ideas about what he/she wants to do. If both of you worked, you are more likely to have a common thought process about what you might want to do relative to your careers. If your partner was a stay-at-home spouse, you must recognize that they too had a career; it's just that you never really paid them for their contributions. They have as much of a right to determine what they want to do in their retirement as you do.

Retirement planning, certainly the initial stages of discussion, are a tremendous opportunity to forge a new bond in a relationship. Some couples may have existed for a number of years or decades without much conversation about the future. You may have had goals for your children or your career but when they were accomplished you may have eased back into a life of routine and failed to truly communicate with each other about the things that you would like to do or accomplish in your retirement.

Retirement offers the opportunity to re-establish an open, honest dialog about what each of you would like to do with the rest of your lives together. Remember, retirement planning must be a team effort.

> *Key Point:* The *process* of determining what you and your partner want to do with the rest of your lives is almost as important as the *actual retirement plan itself.* The retirees who establish an open dialog and talk from their hearts about their wants and needs in retirement are able to accomplish just about anything. Unfortunately there are many dysfunctional retirements because the partners failed to sit down and talk openly and honestly about what they both wanted to do. The process of talking about retirement is the first step to ensuring a successful retirement.

❑ **Focus on Happiness**—retirement should be a time of great happiness and fun. You worked very hard during your career to position yourself for retirement, so make sure you really enjoy the opportunity. Go for it with gusto with a giant smile on your face. Pat yourself on the back, you made it! The fundamental purpose of your PRP is to make sure you do the kind of things that will make you happy. But, remember that happiness is in the eye of the beholder. One person's happiness might be another person's poison. There is no one answer that will fit everyone. Your happiness is very personal. The key is that you need to look inside yourself and determine what you need to do to be happy.

Happiness does not necessarily relate to fame or fortune or some other specific measurement. It is a very personal, internal feeling. For instance, Mother Theresa was a remarkably happy person but she lived a life of servitude and poverty that many people would think was difficult, tedious, and painful. Her happiness was the inner sense of peace and satisfaction she received from helping others.

You will know down deep when you have hit upon your personal understanding of happiness and fulfillment. Sometimes the striving toward a goal is more important than reaching the goal since some goals might not be possible to accomplish or maintain. For instance, all of us want to have a happy, contented family but all we can do is work very hard at making it happen, then hope and pray that it comes about.

❑ **Resolve Past Conflicts**—everyone has done something in their life that may have directly or inadvertently harmed another person or group. It is also true that many people carry these feelings and grudges to their grave. When you consider that you are entering the last quarter of your life, it is time to wipe your slate clean.

In effect, many people need to go to "confession", literally or figuratively. The Catholic Church has the sacrament of reconciliation or confession. It provides a person with an opportunity to get their "sins" off their chest and start afresh.

I went to a Catholic grade school and every Friday we were paraded down to church for confession. Most of us prayed for guidance to come up with yet another creative, new sin of the week. Heavens knows, but not the nuns of the era, that most kids don't sin that much and probably didn't need weekly confessions but I logged enough confessions to last my entire life.

The principle of confession is sound, namely that the act of confessing an inappropriate action is good for the soul. When we confess something that we've done that may have harmed someone else, we get a sense of calm and peace that uplifts our spirit. One of the important things we need to do before we complete the fourth quarter of life is determine what "sins" we need to confess and who we need to forgive or apologize to for our errant actions.

The fact of the matter is that just about all of us have some skeletons in the closet that might involve family members or friends or business associates. All of these skeletons act as a burden on our soul that weighs down our emotional well being. The only way to get rid of these burdens is to eliminate them. Your goal should be to go into retirement without any unnecessary baggage. Therefore, you have to make amends for your past sins, whether they were intentional or not, whether they were your fault or not.

The process is similar to a confession. The big difference is that you don't have to confess your sins to a priest or spiritual advisor, although that might be appropriate for some. You need to put yourself in front of those people who you may have offended, or who offended you, and apologize or seek reconciliation. It's a tough task but something that will allow your spirit to soar and remove any negatives that could prevent you from feeling really good about yourself.

❑ **Capitalize on your experience and wisdom**—an old German proverb says, "We get too soon old and too late smart." The fact is that some people simply get old and never learn from their experiences. Fortunately most of the people I've met over age 60 have developed an innate understanding of human nature because they have learned from their life experiences and have arrived at a condition we call wisdom.

My grandfather used to say that wisdom is the blending of age and experience. He believed that younger people could be really intelligent but they can't be wise because wisdom is the blending of age and experience over a long period of time.

Some of you may not yet realize just how much wisdom you have accumulated in your life or may have relegated it to a lesser status because people around you have stopped asking for your advice and counsel. Unfortunately the culture in the United States is not too senior-friendly. Our culture tends to put seniors on the shelf. Yet other cultures around the world, including most Asian and Native American Indian cultures, put its elders in positions of power and leadership because they value the importance of wisdom.

The collective wisdom that is present in the minds and bodies of our senior citizens is one of the world's biggest and most powerful assets. The problem is that much of the wisdom lies hidden and unused. At a time when the world needs all the help it can get, there is a vast reservoir of wisdom that could be tapped for everyone's benefit. The challenge is to find a way to use your personal storehouse of wisdom and experience to enrich the rest of your life while simultaneously benefiting your family, church, community and mankind.

Your greatest asset is your experience and wisdom, not your net worth. You have to determine how you will use these assets in the last quarter of your life to help you achieve your maximum level of happiness and personal fulfillment. For example, one way to use these personal assets is to volunteer with an organization like SCORE, the Senior Corps of Retired Executives, a program sponsored by the Small Business Administration. The program is staffed by volunteer retired business executives who provide small business owners with advice and counsel based on their personal experience and wisdom.

There are many ways to use your experience and wisdom. All you have to do is search for them.

❑ **Utilize your Strengths**—one of the chapters in the PRP deals with conducting a SWOT analysis. In the corporate world, the acronym "SWOT" stands for Strengths, Weaknesses, Opportunities and Threats. It is a tool used by organizations to plan more effectively by analyzing each of the components of their performance. The intent of creating a SWOT analysis as a part of your PRP is to ensure that you align your existing strengths and capabilities with the opportunities you want to pursue in retirement. In short, find ways to capitalize on your strengths.

For instance, if you are an accomplished carpenter, you can pursue woodworking as a hobby or consider setting up a business to help other homeowners make improvements to their homes. If you play to your strengths, you will not only enjoy what you do, for fun or profit, but you will develop a deep sense of satisfaction and fulfillment, and that's what retirement is all about.

Way back when you started your career, whether it was motivated by your education or degree from high school or college, or area of interest, you probably didn't stop to evaluate your strengths; for instance, by taking an aptitude test. Many of us simply got a job and developed skills and experience a year at a time in a particular occupation or industry. If you went into sales, you learned how to become an excellent salesperson and became an expert on your product line and industry. But underneath all of that practical experience is a person who has unique strengths that might be significantly different than those you used to make a living. Retirement provides you with the opportunity to assess your true strengths and consider getting into something that you are really good at.

For instance, there are a great many successful professional athletes who made their living on the field or in the arena and retired at a relatively early age to pursue a totally different career that aligned with their inherent strengths and capabilities. One notable example is Ken Venturi who retired from competitive golf and became one of the best golf commentators of all time. He was able to communicate with the audience based on his playing experience, yet nothing would lead you to think that a

221

professional golfer, who speaks very little on the golf course, would have latent communication skills.

Key Point: Identify your true, sometimes hidden, talents and strengths to find greater happiness in retirement.

- **Follow Your Dream**—the eighth insight deals with discovering your hidden desires or following your dream. For instance, my mother, God rest her soul, planned for years to make a trip to Italy to visit Rome and the Vatican. She talked about it, envisioned it, prayed for it and promised herself that one day she would do it. Unfortunately she developed a terminal illness and was not able to fulfill her dream. How many dreams or hidden desires have you suppressed for a very long time? How many things have put off indefinitely? How many times have you said that some day, some way you will do something? Hey, all of us have our hidden desires and wishes, you are not unique.

The difference between the truly happy retirees and those who die with unfulfilled dreams is that the happy people stop talking about it and start doing things that make them happy and fulfilled. It's that simple. You need to make a list of all those things that you really, really want to do while you still can. You, and only you, can do it. The important thing is to start. At my mother's funeral I removed the cross from the top of her casket and put it in my suitcase to take to Rome for her and provide her with the experience that she was not able to experience herself.

Key Point: Follow your dream while you are still able. Don't wait for your children to do it for you. If there is something you really want to do, just do it.

❑ **Pass Along Your Lore, Legend and Legacy**—if you have ever sat around a fireside, out in the woods, with your family or a group of friends, it is inevitable that someone will start telling a story, then another and another. Pretty soon everyone is caught up in the rapture and magic of storytelling. One of the great losses of advancing technology has been the gradual erosion of storytelling in our families. Television has overtaken family conversation. As a result we are in grave danger, as a society, of failing to pass along the lore and legend of our present generation and prior generations that we hold in the recesses of our collective memories. Who will tell our children and grandchildren about our experiences? Who will be able to relate, after we are gone, what the world was like when we were kids? Who will communicate with the next generation what life was like before television, cell phones, computers, iPods, Blackberries, faxes, texting, copy machines, calculators, supersonic transportation, space exploration, organ transplants, CDs and DVDs, microwaves, air conditioning, automatic transmissions, etc. etc.

The fact is that the senior generation has experienced things that our grandchildren don't even comprehend. It is our job to pass along our lore and legend so that they will be able to tell their children and grandchildren what their grandparents told them. It's the Roots thing up close and personal.

The greatest legacy that any of us could leave is the unification and solidification of our individual family units. The best way to unify and solidify our families is through communication. We can only do that while we are alive. One of your key roles as the patriarch or matriarch of your family is to take the lead in passing along the lore and legend of your generation.

Key Point: Turn off the TVs when you are with your children and grandchildren. Gather them around and begin to tell them everything you can remember about your life. Pass along your heritage and the memorable events of your life. They will be enthralled and you will create a lasting and tender legacy.

❏ **Remember Your Purpose**—most business plans have an exit strategy that describes how the owners of the business hope to get their investment from the business when they decide to sell, leave or retire. Similarly, you need to have an exit strategy that allows you to spell out your personal wishes and preferences for how you want things to be handled after you are gone. The last step in creating your PRP is to develop your own personal exit strategy. Before you get into those details, this last guideline to retirement planning involves the need to remember your purpose in life. Regardless of your religious preference, even if you profess to no particular religious beliefs, retirement provides you with the opportunity to reflect on the true purpose of life and how you feel about your overall accomplishments. If you are satisfied with what you have done, simply continue on your path. If you feel you need to do more to achieve a better sense of purpose, then you need to make a commitment to identify the things you would still like to do and include them in your PRP.

Most people believe there is also a higher purpose in life. From a religious perspective, the greatest commandment of all is to love thy God with thy whole heart and soul, and to love thy neighbor as thyself for the love of God. If you believe this commandment and accept that someday you will be judged by a higher being on all that you've done or failed to do, you should then be able to make an assessment if you have achieved, or hope to achieve your true purpose in life based on the greatest commandment.

Key Point: the Bible says, "What does it profit a man if he gains the entire world but suffers the loss of his immortal soul." ~Mark 8:36. Your accomplishments in life are your legacy. If they include an understanding of and commitment to the greatest commandment, you have lived a truly purposeful life. If you still need to do more to achieve your true purpose, you then know what you have to do in retirement to achieve your goal.

In a nutshell, the purpose of these ten insights is to help you create the appropriate attitude about retirement planning. The actual PRP process will walk you through the ten steps that are the components of the plan itself. If you understand the ten principles above, you will be more readily able to start your actual PRP.

Chapter 22

Epilog
Words of Wisdom

When I started to write *Retirement Renaissance*, I was in the process of trying to figure out why I wasn't totally enthused with retirement. After the book was written, I stepped back to see if I could identify what I really learned from the experience. The insights in the previous chapter were extremely valuable in establishing the proper perspective and understanding the challenges and opportunities in retirement.

After rereading the insights and thinking about what meant the most to me, there are nine insights that are the most important words of wisdom that I could pass along to any new or recently retired senior.

❑ There is a *difference between financial planning and retirement planning.* Whether or not you built a substantial financial nest egg that will allow you to live comfortably in retirement, your retirement planning is only half done. It is vital that you also plan for all the other issues and contingencies that were outlined in the Ten Steps. The key point is that financial planning is only one important component of a comprehensive retirement plan.

❑ There is *no such thing as a universal retirement plan* that works for everyone. A retirement plan is highly personal based on the unique wants and needs of both planning partners. What makes one person or couple happy and content in retirement might drive someone else up the wall.

❑ Many seniors are *not prepared to cope with the psychological impact of retirement.* The post-retirement syndrome is a reality that is triggered by the inability of retirees to replace the rewards and gratification that was previously provided by their jobs and career. If you don't replace this need, you will not be happy in retirement.

❑ It is *vital that you take good care of your body and mind in retirement.* There is a clear-cut link between happiness and longevity for retirees that exercise their bodies and minds regularly and routinely. The mantra of a healthy retiree is, "Use it or lose it!"

❑ *You have an obligation to prepare your "exit strategy"* for your partner and family. Everyone needs a last will and testament, and advance directives especially a living will, and detailed instructions about your personal preferences. You must also have a competent attorney and financial planner to assist in preparing these vital documents.

❑ *Retirement planning is a mutual process.* It is important that both partners have equal input in the retirement discussions. Retirement can be the best years of your life or the worst if the partners have different points of view about retirement preferences. Perhaps the quote by author Ella Harris puts the issue in perspective, *"A retired husband is often a wife's full-time job."*

❑ *It is never too late to follow your dreams.* Many seniors end up at the doorstep to retirement with a good many unfulfilled dreams. The reality is that there are only so many years left to do whatever it is that has motivated you throughout your entire life. Don't put off your dreams. As Nike says, "Just do it!"

❑ *Attitude is everything.* Anybody over the age of 50 needs to realize that they are sliding down the other side of the mountain of life. If you think you are old, you will act like you are old. If you think you are young of heart, you will act and feel young at heart. It's all a matter of attitude.

❑ Lastly, *never forget your purpose.* When all is said and done, the true measure of success and fulfillment is not material possessions or power and prestige, it is simply that you tried to be a good person, a full and complete person. Whether you are spiritual or not, you can never forget that life is short and eternity is forever. One day you will be judged on what you did, not on who you were.

You have the opportunity to do whatever you want to do in retirement. The most important thing is that you have to plan for what you want to do, especially how to deal with the psychological loss of your job and career and the sense of wellbeing and self-esteem it provided.

Retirement will not wait for you, it will happen whether you are prepared or not. Just follow my advice and prepare a retirement plan, with your spouse or partner. I guarantee that you will thank me in a few years from now.

Incidentally, after I wrote the book, I decided to go back to work, part-time, because I really enjoyed to work. My present guideline about work is that I will continue as long as two things are present; first, that my clients continue to think that I can add value; and second, that I am willing to roll out of bed in the morning and go to work. When either or both of these guidelines aren't there, I will retire, again.

Chapter 23

The Age of Wisdom

"A truly wise man is the one who knows what he knows and knows what he doesn't know and has the wisdom to understand the difference."   *~Anonymous*

Peace Corps

On March 1, 1961, President John F. Kennedy signed an executive order establishing the Peace Corps. Three days later, Sargent Shriver was appointed its first Director. In July, Peace Corps assignments were planned for Ghana, Tanzania, Colombia, the Philippines, Chile, and St. Lucia. More than 5,000 applicants took the first exams, required at the time to enter the Peace Corps. The first group of 51 Volunteers departed that year for Ghana.

Since then, over 178,000 Americans have served as Peace Corps Volunteers in 138 countries. Their individual experiences, in villages, towns, and cities around the world, have composed a legacy of service that has become part of America's history.

The Peace Corps has had perhaps a far greater positive impact on foreign policy than any program in our history. It was a new, bold concept that energized the country and made everyone proud to be an American. The Peace Corps transcended bi-partisan politics and became one of the few major government programs that had support on both sides of the aisle in Congress and throughout the world. Nobody has ever criticized the Peace Corps about their mission, goals and strategies.

The Peace Corps is a wonderful example of how a global concept can work for the benefit of all mankind.

If the Peace Corps can have such a positive, enduring impact on our global society, why can't we find a way to use the stored-up wisdom in the minds of our senior citizens around the world to solve major challenges and make the world a safer and far better place to live?

The concept could be called "The Wisdom Corps."

As a new retiree, you will be joining a global alliance of men and women who have a significant characteristic in common, namely the achievement of a state or condition we call wisdom. I hope by reading about wisdom it will inspire you to use this precious resource in your retirement for your betterment and that of your spouse, partner, family, and global community.

The dictionary defines wisdom as "the faculty of making the best use of knowledge, experience and understanding." I believe there is a strong linkage between wisdom and age. My Grandfather said it this way, "When a person is young they can be really intelligent, but they can't be wise because wisdom is the result of age and experience working together over a long period of time."

Older people possess a great deal of innate wisdom that they accumulated during the course of experiencing the joys and frustrations of life. Wisdom is present in many forms and shapes. Some people are wise in their occupational or educational specialties, others are wise about the way things work, and still others have a wonderful facility to understand the intricacies of human relationships. Just about every senior is able to help younger people make up their mind about important issues because they have been there, done that and intuitively know the most desirable course of action.

The wisdom that is resident in the minds and experiences of all seniors represents one of the greatest untapped potentials in the world. The distilled wisdom of seniors is waiting to be discovered and utilized. Unfortunately the world does not understand or identify with this powerful resource.

The problem is that most contemporary cultures no longer honor their seniors and their accumulated wisdom as they did in prior generations. The contemporary culture of the 21st century appears to align more with youth than with age.

For instance, in past times and cultures the elders in a culture were placed in positions of honor and respect. They were the leaders and decision-makers. They were the source of lore and legend. They provided the community with stability and direction. Many times the elders were able to maintain their calm and cool while the younger members of the community were willing to fight and die for a cause that the elders were able to resolve without conflict.

Consider the past generations of the American Indians, the Eskimos, the cultures in the Far East, Middle East and many of the cultures in Europe; they all placed a high value on the wisdom of their elders. This understanding was passed along to the immigrants of America and persevered for several generations. These cultures recognized that their elders provided a sense of perspective on life that younger people had not yet developed.

When I was a young boy I remember that my grandfather, a strict German disciplinarian, was the true patriarch of the extended family. Everyone sought out his advice, counsel, and permission, much like was portrayed in the movie *The Godfather*. No one in the family made a major decision without first discussing it with grandfather. After the discussion, he would put his hands on the younger person's head and then bless them with a sign of approval and good luck.

Most of the immigrants to the United States experienced a similar family experience. Sadly it has all but disappeared in less than a century. Few ethnic groups or families or social groups use the wisdom of their elders to make important decisions. Ironically, it has happened during a time when there are more seniors than ever before.

The world of today not only fails to use the wisdom and experience of its seniors, but the seniors are metaphorically put out to pasture when they retire. The prevailing attitude among younger people is that they no longer need the advice and counsel of seniors. The age of technology and advanced education has apparently preempted the importance of wisdom. Yet the major advancements of the past 50 years were created and introduced by the retired generation.

The Irony of Retirement

There is an interesting and sad irony about retirement. It takes decades for a person to become really good at their career or profession and to accumulate a high level of experience and wisdom. Then suddenly when they reach age 55 or 60 or 65, the prevailing mind-set of our modern culture suggests that it is time for them to get out of the way and move into retirement. Granted, there are lots of retirees who are ready to take leave of their career, but the irony is that most seniors leave their career at a time when they are nearing the peak of their skills, capabilities, and wisdom.

Wisdom is one of the few things in life that gets better with age. The more experience a person has and the longer they live and remain active, the more wisdom they accumulate. Why would anyone want to put a strong player on the bench when they are at the top of their game? The reason is simple: our culture no longer respects or feels the need to use the experience and wisdom of its elders.

The failure to use this powerful resource is also a waste of money. If you want to look at it from an investment point of view, the company or institution that employs a senior could receive their greatest return on their investment by allowing their seniors to continue using their wisdom to address the really tough issues.

For instance, my wife had an uncle who worked in a giant glass making plant in Detroit. He repaired the massive glass-making machines and over the years developed an intimate understanding about their peculiarities. He became so experienced about the machines that when the company expanded internationally, they asked this blue-collar mechanic to go around the world to help the educated plant engineers install the glass-making machines.

Just think about the value of the wisdom that is stored inside the average retiree. One way to put a dollar figure on the experience and wisdom of a long time employee is to add up the compensation and benefits over their entire career. The number is a small estimate of their net worth to the company, or the value of bringing in a replacement. The failure to utilize this resource is the equivalent of taking a valuable asset out of production.

I don't imply that people should never retire. Whether a senior is anxious to retire or extremely reticent, the issue is not when a person retires, the issue is to determine how the company or institution uses the wisdom for their benefit and for the satisfaction of the prospective retiree. Why ignore or waste this precious and valuable asset?

History is replete with examples of men and women who made some of their greatest contributions when they were in the prime of their "wisdom" years. Examples include Thomas Jefferson, Mother Teresa, Benjamin Franklin, Mohandas Gandhi, Michelangelo, Thomas Edison, Helen Keller, Henry Ford, Albert Einstein, Winston Churchill, Rosa Parks, Nelson Mandela, Leonardo DaVinci, Susan B. Anthony, Franklin D. Roosevelt, Jimmy Carter, Boris Pasternak, Maya Angelou, Bob Hope, Ernest Hemingway, Eleanor Roosevelt, Ronald Reagan, Billy Graham, Sam Walton, Walt Disney, Pope John Paul II, to name a few.

If all of these people had settled into retirement and spent their days relaxing in the sun, many of the world's greatest accomplishments would never have happened. Many of their endeavors were made possible as a direct result of the wisdom they developed throughout their lives.

Our contemporary culture is at a critical juncture: as more and more seniors are retiring, the challenges in the world intensify. Why can't we find a way to use the wisdom of our seniors to help resolve some of these challenges whether they are at home, in a business or institution, or a government or a church?

The Challenge

The first step is to recognize the need to use the wisdom of our senior citizens. Who better could address the local and global challenges than the millions of retired seniors who have been left out of the loop because they are "retired"?

The next step is to find a way to encourage and reward seniors for providing their wisdom and experience. Many institutions and organizations have created barriers that prevent seniors from contributing advice and counsel. For instance, when a person retires from a company they are literally cut-off from active participation in activities that they were once deeply involved in. If there were a way to keep retirees tied to performance and results, it is possible that the environment of retirement might allow some people to accelerate their creative juices and identify possible new solutions or approaches. There is no need to shut out this kind of experience and wisdom.

It might be appropriate to provide retirees with some type of ongoing incentive for coming up with new ideas in their retirement. It would bind people to the company or institution and provide an invaluable resource that could serve as a rather unique competitive differentiation.

From my consulting days I recall when we would try to impress a potential client with a calculation of the vast number of years of experience we had on our team for solving a particular type of problem. If companies and institutions followed a similar approach and utilized the power of their retirees' experience base, they could overwhelm their competition with credentials and actual years of experience and wisdom.

If programs could be developed that would allow retirees to participate in some manner in their former careers or other areas of need, the same approach could be used to address more serious areas of national and global needs.

I believe that every business, institution, organization and government would benefit from the free-flow of experience and wisdom that is resident in the minds and experience base of our retired senior population. This represents a tremendous opportunity to create some type of structure that would organize and implement programs to serve as the vehicle for bringing the two sides together.

For instance, there is an organization within the Small Business Administration called SCORE that stands for Service Corps Of Retired Executives and has become the "Counselors for America's Small Businesses." Over 50 years ago a group of retired executives got together and volunteered to help small businesses solve their growth and operational problems. The group provides a wide range of services to thousands of small business owners. They are one excellent example about how a group of senior retirees were able to use their experience and wisdom to help fellow entrepreneurs.

I believe there is a need for an expanded national and global concept that would help other types of institutions, organizations and governments. If we could harness and categorize the experience base of millions of seniors, the database would have every conceivable qualification and credential to address every imaginable problem. The concept is the **Wisdom Corps**.

The only thing lacking is the commitment and the organization to do it.

Let's fast forward and imagine that we were able to develop a concept and an organizational structure that used the wisdom resources of our seniors at the local and national level. The next step is to think about expanding the concept to a global perspective. Try to imagine an organization of seniors who would be dedicated to helping solve the problems and challenges of our global society. Would that not be a noble and worthwhile idea?

The timing is right for the creation of a bold, new concept that molds together two converging needs: the first is the need to utilize the collective wisdom power of our seniors and the second is the need to find new and innovative solutions for our local, national and global challenges and opportunities.

At the local or national level, companies and institutions need to find ways to be more effective and efficient in their ability to compete and deliver goods and services. At the global level, the problems that need to be addressed include poverty, starvation in under-developed countries, the AIDS epidemic, global warming, terrorism, nuclear proliferation, war, dictatorship, genocide, and the on-going territorial disputes.

The concept of using the accumulated wisdom of our seniors to address problems is a pretty lofty idea, but is there any problem that could not be solved if we put our collective minds to it and really wanted to find a solution?

Is it also not possible that the bringing together of seniors to solve problems could become the vehicle to improve relationships at all levels of our global society? It is usually true that people are able to get along together, regardless of race or ethicality, when they set aside political, ethnic, and territorial issues. Could it be that the seniors of the world might become the peacemakers of our generation?

If we were able to harness the wisdom of all seniors and focus it on solving problems, is it also not possible that future generations will look back and refer to this period of history as "The Wisdom Generation?" It was a time when the seniors of the world created a true Retirement Renaissance.

Join the Renaissance...Enjoy your retirement!

About the Author

 I am a retiree, a veteran retiree. I am a regular, run of the mill kind of senior citizen. I was a management consultant in my career, I still work and teach part-time, but none of my prior experience had anything to do with retirement planning. My credentials for writing the book are based solely on personal retirement experience. The theory behind the book is simple: if you want medical advice, go to a doctor; if you want legal advice, go to an attorney; if you want retirement advice, you should go to a veteran retiree.

I was born and grew up in Dayton, OH but relocated to Atlanta in 1979. I was the only boy in a family of four. My mother was a single mom after my dad died in a tragic accident. She was an elementary school teacher. I was born about ten years before the Baby Boomer generation. I graduated from Chaminade High School, the University of Dayton with a B.S. in Business Administration, and an M.B.A. from Xavier University in Cincinnati.

I am married to my first and only wife, Patty, a Registered Nurse by profession and mother and grandmother extraordinaire by practice. We have five adult children, four boys and a girl, and five grandsons. Our oldest and youngest sons were born, unexpectedly, with multiple handicaps, including mental retardation, cerebral palsy and vision problems. We cared for both sons with the help of our other children for over 30 years in our home and learned a great deal about the challenges and blessings of caring for two of God's very special children. It has transformed our lives and we are blessed to have been involved for over four decades with various organizations that provide much needed services for all the special people of the world.

Our family was featured on the *Phil Donahue Show* many years ago in a program entitled *The Exceptional Children.* The title came from a comment we made to Phil when he asked us what it was like to care for not one, but two, handicapped sons. We responded that we never thought of our sons as being handicapped, a somewhat negative term. We think of our sons as being *exceptional.*

Although our lives have been defined by the experiences with our special sons, we take comfort in the fact that our sons have been responsible for causing countless other parents to thank God for the many things that we all tend to take for granted. No one knows the plight of the parents of special needs children better than the parents of these children. Many parents and sons and daughters have told us that our acceptance of God's will and our family's commitment to our special sons has been an inspiration and has caused them to put their challenges in perspective.

One of my motivations in writing the book was to include the need to go beyond traditional retirement planning and make provisions for our special needs sons after we are gone. It is a problem that faces all the parents of special needs children. There comes a time when a special child can no longer be cared for by aging parents. We were fortunate to have anticipated the problem and were able to have our sons placed in residential homes managed by United Cerebral Palsy Association where they receive professional care and compassionate attention from a dedicated staff on a 24/7 basis. During the day, our sons attend the DeKalb County, GA, Training Center Program that is dedicated to helping over 200 adult special needs citizens achieve their maximum potential. We feel comfortable that our sons will be well cared for after we are gone because our other children will continue to work with the organizations that have been a part of our lives for all these many years. Good luck on your retirement journey.

~Bill Clarke, Author

Contact Information

The book is available commercially through
eBook and conventional booksellers under
Retirement Renaissance
ISBN: 978-1-61623-893-3

For additional information about the book,
how to contact the author,
or to place a direct order, go to:

www.retirementren.com

and follow the links, or send an email to:

info@retirementren.com

Index

CPSIA information can be obtained at www.ICGtesting.com
Printed in the USA
LVOW121022110113

315304LV00001B/9/P